HOW YOU SEE YOU

Emerald Lewis

BALBOA.
PRESS

A DIVISION OF HAY HOUSE

Scripture taken from the King James Version of the Bible.

Scripture quotations marked (NIV) are taken from the Holy Bible, New International Version®, NIV®. Copyright © 1973, 1978, 1984, 2011 by Biblica, Inc.™ Used by permission of Zondervan. All rights reserved worldwide. www. zondervan.com The "NIV" and "New International Version" are trademarks registered in the United States Patent and Trademark Office by Biblica, Inc.™

Balboa Press books may be ordered through booksellers or by contacting:

Balboa Press
A Division of Hay House
1663 Liberty Drive
Bloomington, IN 47403
www.balboapress.com
1 (877) 407-4847

Because of the dynamic nature of the Internet, any web addresses or links contained in this book may have changed since publication and may no longer be valid. The views expressed in this work are solely those of the author and do not necessarily reflect the views of the publisher, and the publisher hereby disclaims any responsibility for them.

The author of this book does not dispense medical advice or prescribe the use of any technique as a form of treatment for physical, emotional, or medical problems without the advice of a physician, either directly or indirectly. The intent of the author is only to offer information of a general nature to help you in your quest for emotional and spiritual well-being. In the event you use any of the information in this book for yourself, which is your constitutional right, the author and the publisher assume no responsibility for your actions.

Any people depicted in stock imagery provided by Thinkstock are models, and such images are being used for illustrative purposes only. Certain stock imagery © Thinkstock.

Print information available on the last page.

ISBN: 978-1-5043-9342-3 (sc)
ISBN: 978-1-5043-9343-0 (e)

Balboa Press rev. date: 12/13/2017

Contents

*I AM THE IMAGE AND
LIKENESS OF GOD*

*I AM BLESSED AND
CANNOT BE CURSED*

Prayer For Submitting

Heavenly father in heaven, creator of everything seen and unseen; in the name of Jesus Christ I want to thank you for the breath of life and the breath to say thank you.

I humbly come to you with a humble spirit. Heavenly father I am submitting myself to you, asking you for the spirit of discernment, the spirit of wisdom, the spirit of understanding, the spirit of knowledge, the spirit of strength, the spirit of wisdom, and the spirit of love to love each other through the spirit of our Lord and savior Jesus Christ.

I pray that your Holy Spirit will power me, fill me, lead me and guide me through this life in the name of Jesus Christ.

I pray for the strength to resist the devil and his evil followers; so that they will flee. Heavenly father cover everyone that is reading this message with the blood of your son Jesus Christ. Lord open their spirit, their heart, and their mind to receive your love.

Lord I pray that no weapon form against us shall prosper and any tongue that speak against us shall not prosper. In the name of Jesus Christ, I pray.

Heavenly father I pray the promise that you make through Abraham, that anyone who bless us, you shall bless them, and anyone that curse us you shall curse them.

I pray that your will be done. I pray that your light will shine through every heart and spirit cleansing them and setting them free from the spirit of the world. In the name of Jesus Christ.

I pray that every tongue will confess, and that their heart and mind will be filled with your peace, love and joy.

Jehovah-jireh my God shall supply all my needs according to his riches in Glory he will give his angels charge over me. The Lord is our provider. May everyone who is reading the message be bless from the beginning to the end of this book. Emmanuel God is with us. God bless our eyes.

Unity In One

1 Corinthians 12:12-13 (NIV) the human body has many parts, but the many parts make up one whole body. Therefore, it is with the body of Christ.

Some of us are Jews some are gentiles, some are slaves and some are free. Nevertheless, we have all been baptized into one body by one spirit, and we all share the same spirit.

We Are The Beauty Of God Image Within

I see me for who I am in Christ Jesus, and the way Christ see me is the way I see my life; I am the image and likeness of God, Beautiful, loving, kind, caring, and full of joy, happiness and much more of his blessings. Life is so beautiful; if you look, you will see its beauty.

Moreover, finding faith within Gods words, where his light is shining, his wind is blowing, his rain is falling and his love keeps coming our way.

Every day I live my life with the love God has and still putting into my heart. Likewise, living to please the Christ within me, the God in me, the Christ in me is the one who gives me the strength to live my everyday life.

Trying my best and doing what I can, letting my heavenly father do the rest. I let the Lord carry me, when and where he leads me I will follow. The light of my heavenly father always shines into my heart, bringing me joy, comfort, love, happiness and peace. I love you Lord, thank you.

When the Lord speaks, I listen. When I do not listen, I get to find out the hard way. The Lord gave us all free will of choice and choices to make, sometimes we make choices and we have to live with the results from them.

There are many things the bible speaks about and I have seen some of them with my own eyes happening. I know the Lord is my shepherd, my rock, my light and everything I need on my every day journey; moreover, the Lord is always there for you and for me. I can say I know how much the Lord loves and cares for you and me.

We are living in a world where most people and things look alike and seem real but it is not. It is only real, when seeing with the eyes of Christ; when I say seeing not with the flesh but with the spirit. God do not speak to the flesh, he speaks to the spirit. Trust no one but Christ our Lord. Jesus spoke these words, I will never leave you nor forsaken you.

The flesh will let you down because it always wants what it sees. I have experience so many things with people; many of them will try any and everything to get their way, and to put you down. Not everything you see and hear is real or true.

The truth is inside the words of God, and that is where your strength comes from, the source of life. People are good at what they do and say, but our heavenly father is best, he is our light; the light to shine the way for us to see through his son Jesus Christ.

Do not let anyone deceive you in his or her lies. 2 Corinthians 11:13-16 (NIV) these people are false apostles. They are deceitful workers who disguise themselves as apostles of Christ. But I am surprises! Even Satan disguises himself as an angel of light.

Therefore, it is no wonder that his servants also disguise themselves as servants of righteousness. In the end, they will get the punishment their wicked deeds deserve.

There are many wolves in sheep clothing. They are just waiting for a chance, an invitation. No one can come in unless you invite him or her, furthermore opening the door for him or her to come in.

John 8:12 (NIV) Jesus spoke to the people once more and said," I am the light of the world. If you follow me, you will not have to walk in darkness, because you will have the light that leads to life.

The only door you should open is the door for Christ our Lord to enter; he will shine and make a way for you. He is the way the truth and the life. Let the Lord Take deep root into your heart, spirit and soul; likewise watering the Christ so he can grow stronger in you.

A tree without strong roots will never stand. When the wind blows, it will fall. The deeper the roots, the stronger and taller the tree will be. I am the vine, and you are the branches. That is the spoken words of our Lord Jesus Christ.

Anyone who comes to me hungry or thirsty, I will give them food and rest for their soul. They will never go hungry or thirsty again. Likewise seeing with the third eye, the inner source of creation, of life and love; living with nature, by the words that come from the mouth of God, and by action of faith and love.

Moreover, cleaning the inside, make sure it stays clean and pure, the inside and outside of the cup. The heart lives long, just like the blood when it runs like water into our veins. The breath of life is all we can take, gradually, day by day. That is why we should pray and ask the Lord to provide us our daily bread and give us day by day to do his will.

Head And Not The Tail

Deuteronomy 28:13 (KJV) And the Lord shall make you the head, and not the tail; and you shall be above only, and you shall not be beneath; if that you hearken unto the commandments of the Lord your God, which I command you this day, to observe and to do them:

Furthermore, keeping our heads looking up into the sky, feeling the vibration of the rain falling purifying our soul. Saying no darkness can cover our light, walking into the valley of the shadow of death having no fear but only faith in Christ. Indeed knowing the Lord Rod and staff will protect us from all evil.

The source of one in oneself always guides and protects the eye to see and to follow the light to the pathway of the truth. The head is now out of the lion mouth, and the head of the serpent is crushed; it is not the end, it is just the beginning.

Facing life as it comes, just like the waves beating among itself; watching the rising of the sun, shining from one end of the earth to the next.

Making a way to the moon, love is floating in the air falling upon the just and the unjust. Mouth open with no words, heart beating with the sounds of joy and a positive vibes.

So many people invited them self into my circle, trying to put darkness into my light. I do not know who they are, where they came from and where they are going. Riding them out like a bicycle.

How you see you, beautiful from the inside shining out. Moreover, being who you are, not who they say you are. Nevertheless, who Christ said you are a tree by the fruit it bears.

Furthermore, holding the key for oneself in thy own hands, searching every an anywhere still cannot find. Lost souls knocking on their own door, no one can let you in but your own. Changing the way we think, the things we do and say. Now seeing freedom from the obsessive and scary thoughts, taking control as the wind blows its negative energy away.

Likewise seeing the sun shining through the clouds with the thought of love. I began Planting and sowing new seeds as we reap the recovery of its joy. Therefore, change in one self, makes everything around you change. Moreover, taking back your power from who you are not, to who you are.

Living from the heart; likewise leading thy own life with the help from the source of life. Looking behind me to see thy own shadow, however trying to run away; but there is no way to escape but to face thy own self.

The joy, love, peace and strength of the Lord live in my spirit and soul. Sheltering and showing me his goodness and mercy, as it follows me all the days of my life, as I dwell in the house of the Lord forever.

The most high lives in me, listening to the echo of thy heart as nature calls. Standing and fighting for the rights of thy own life. Now war started popping up ever where like popcorn, searching for peace.

Thy kingdom comes to quench the thirst of the burning fire inside, Building thy house on the rock close to the sea. As I watch the waves covering, and sinking anything in its way. Just like the negative thoughts, creeping into the mind like a thief.

Moreover, catching him or her before they take root; no squatter in thy land. Seeing thy own reflection in the water looking back, saying let me help you help me. Seeing thy self… walking, in the desert, looking for a place to rest into the arms of the earth.

It feels good to connect with where you come from. Seeing the enemies like a mirage in the desert. Trying to take me away as the winds blow; holding the sands of the desert in my hands, watching how it passes through my fingers, like a tornado.

Taking whatever it likes and disappearing like vapor. The armor, the wings, the love and the armies of the Lord, shelters and protects me always. My soul shouts, I am born again.

My soul rejoices with the joy of the Lord. Saying no weapon form against me shall ever prosper. My heart overcomes the fear of the world, faithfully and triumphantly. I will never give up thy faith; thy faith will live and dies with me.

I was looking at thy chain, to see if there is any weak links. I began traveling on thy journey to live and to complete thy cycle. When I was looking through the eye of a needle, I saw the hands that anointed thy Head with oil. It was covering me and taking root into thy own soil.

I saw the hole they have dug for me slowly they fell into it; Darkness came out, it was trying to make a way for itself. Then suddenly I saw and hear the sound of the lightening saying not today, this one belong to me.

My spirit shout with a loud voice saying no weapon form against me shall ever prosper, I am bless and cannot be curse. The joy of the Lord is my strength; the Lord is my rock and my protection. Whom shall I fear? Running the enemies out like the philistines when a gust of wind came and blow them away.

How you see you now grateful and bless for thy protection, the multitude of light and love shinning and covering thy heart. I am trying to make a way, from the programing minds and the controlling people in the world.

Likewise staying far away from the illusion of others and the things in the world. These things in the world will only make you, seem like you are lost. Our heads was place on our shoulder, for a reason; likewise, our heart was made for a reason also. I let the Spirit of the Lord in my heart intercede for me.

Furthermore, being the captain of thy own ship sailing on the red sea overcoming the battles of fear. Knowing your history and your root where you came from, and where you are going.

Anchoring thy trust in the source of life with the love of Christ Jesus our Lord; living and experiencing thy own life. The motive of thy heart is to succeed, looking at the motive of others trying to succeed by envying thy own brothers and sisters.

Keeping my eyes on the Lord and his promises; guarding thy heart of joy and love, from the evil one and the evil in the world. Experiencing, and enjoy the fruits and love from our creator.

Encouraging thy self to be positive full of love, faith, joy, hope and integrity no matter what may happen. Furthermore, being a fighter, not a victim of thy own life. I am being grateful, for the breath of life, and the gift of love, to love one another with the love of the Lord.

Giving to the poor, and helping the ones in need, looking down from above to help the weak. Giving expecting nothing in return; Giving from a heart of love.

Seeing the ones who give, only what they have to spare. Living in a world, where everything reveals itself. The rich getting richer and the poor crying out for help. Think before you open your mouth.

Romans 12: 7-8-9 (NIV) If your gift is serving others, serve them well. If you are a teacher, teach well. If your gift is to encourage others, be encouraging. If it is giving, give generously. If God has given you leadership ability, take the responsibility seriously. In addition, if you have a gift for showing kindness to others, do it gladly. Don't just pretend to love others. Really, love them. Hate what is wrong. Hold tightly to what is good.

As my heart beats the words of my Lord, saying it is harder for a rich man to enter the kingdom of God, and easier for a camel to pass through the eye of a needle.

Looking at everything, as it is being seduced by the world; awaiting the big trees to enter, as a small axe cuts them down. I came into the world with nothing, but only with God love and I will be leaving with nothing but with his love.

Dust was turned into life, dust as my clothing, and my body as my vehicle. I am living amongst hypocrites, who say they are my friends. They talk in my face and stab me in my back. Naked I came in to this world, and naked I will leave. Time will tell, only fools walk in darkness.

A lamp with no oil, a head with no eyes, and a body with no light. Feeding and nourishing the spirit, so the flesh will not take over. The flesh is weak, and the spirit is willing. The angels from God will guide and protect me from all danger, and dangerous people.

False prophets are shooting up everywhere like plants, trying to make a way for their own self. Corinthians 4:4 (NIV) Satan, who is the god of this world, has blinded the minds of those who do not believe. They are unable to see the glorious light of the good news. They do not understand this message about the glory of Christ, who is the exact likeness of God.

I was knocking until the door was open; I was seeking until I found the way to our Lord. I was asking until I got an answer. The floodgate of heaven opened up and showers of blessing, began washing and shining light into my pathway of life. My spirit was saying to never give up thy faith in Christ.

I was blind, but now I can see. I was deaf, but now I can hear. The songs from the angles of the heavens singing give thanks and praises to the creator.

Revelation 4: 11 (NIV) you are worthy, O Lord our God, to receive glory and honor and power. For you created all things, and they exit because you created what you please.

Revelation 5:12 (NIV) and they sang in a mighty chorus: "worthy is the Lamb who was slaughtered to receive power and riches and wisdom and strength and honor and glory and blessing.

Acts 4:12 (NIV) there is salvation in no one else! God has given no other name under heaven given by which we must be saved.

A Prayer To Our Heavenly Father

Thank you heavenly father, creator of the universe heaven and earth. Thank you for the breath of life and for every day you have brought before my eyes. It is your will in me, Lord forgive me and have mercy on me in the mighty name of you son Jesus Christ I pray.

Blessed be your Holy name Lord, all the glory the honor and praises to you on high. Lord breathe your Holy Spirit on me, therefore I may be filled with your light of love and faith. Lord continue to guide every step I take and make. Lord let your light shine before and in front of me everywhere, I may go.

Fill my heart Lord with the words to say and give me the strength to do thy will to stay faithful. Let your joy be my strength and your peace be my comfort Lord.

Lord you are all I need, the door of my heart is open for you to come in, as I make you my Lord and savior. I am grateful and thankful for life; and for all that, you are giving and doing for me.

I feel so blessed knowing that you love and care for me, even when I did wrong, blessed is your Holy name. Lord as long as you give me the breath of life, day by day to be humble in my spirit. I will praise and believe in you always as long as I live.

In Jesus Christ name, I pray, heavenly father that you will fill me with your love, strength, joy, peace, wisdom, faith, hope and understanding to dwell in your words, your house of love and dwelling shelter with action. In Jesus Christ name, I pray amen.

How You See You, A Person With Patience

Proverbs 16:32 (KJV) He that is slow to anger is better than the mighty; and he that ruleth his spirit than he that taketh a city.

Many of us say we have patience, but when we ask for something and we do not get it right away, or it may get delay; now our patience is tested, what will we do. In addition, how do we react to things in life? Patience is the key to humble your spirit.

Lord my soul and spirit long to be with you; my spirit awaits your love and peace with joy and patience, Lord your joy is what gives me the strength with the living water within my spirit and soul.

I Am Connected To The True Vine

John 15:5 (NIV) Yes I am the vine; you are the branches. Those who remain in me, and I in them, will produce much fruit. For apart from me you can do nothing.

A real education will not teach you to compete; it will teach you how to share and how to love one another. Furthermore, real beauty is never created by you, but only through you; greater is he who lives in you and me is greater than the one in the world.

We are all trees planted by the river of living water; waiting the result of what seeds has been sowed to see what we will reap.

Likewise, beauty only shines in the presence; in and through the eyes and heart of the beholder. Our Lord Jesus Christ lives within you and me with the Holy Spirit; only when you and me are reborn, born again. He is greater in you and me than the things in the world.

In addition, we may feel what we cannot see, and we may see what we cannot feel. Nevertheless, who feels it knows it. God will never put you where he would not take you out. He will never lead you and forsake you; neither will he leave you or forsaken you, he will guard, guide, love and protect you. Christ unfailing love is in and around you and me forever and ever.

Life is so beautiful with the company and love from God and with his sweet fellowship in Christ Holy Spirit. The Holy Spirit is the one that filled up the dark world with light; Jesus Christ the light of the world.

When we continue to praise the father in thanksgiving and in the Spirit, we will get to see more of the glory of our Lord Jesus Christ. Do not say tomorrow I will praise and give thanks, do it today with the breath of life.

The now is not that hard to live in; there may be a difference in living in the present moment.

Example the body is here now, but where is the mind. Love is like a river that never stops flowing, likewise from father to the son; from the mountain into the sea.

Moreover, from a seed that was planted into the ground. It had to die before it slowly turns into a plant or a tree. A beautiful tree planted by the river of living water.

James 3:18 (KIV) and the fruit of righteousness is sown in peace of them that make peace. How can you practice joy, happiness, peace and love? It cannot be practice; all you have to do is allowed it to happen.

We are all investors in something or things, many of us invest in the things that keep us in captivity, things that restrain us and imprison us.

Furthermore, we work so hard to become the way we are; it is all about choice and choices we make; and the words that we speak. Moreover, misery is hard work; it is a choice to be miserable. We have to be working very hard to keep it going. We are so afraid to let go of misery; it seem like we get so used to it, we forget and it becomes part of our life style. Misery is an investment to many people.

The one that is of the world creates misery; moreover, bliss comes by believing and accepting the name of our Lord Jesus Christ. Furthermore being who God created you and me to be.

The more we experience life in the word of the God of our Lord Jesus Christ; the more we become more mature. Likewise, we get to face the things in life that we may fear, by the grace and faith in Christ Jesus our Lord we are overcomers. The best feeling in life is, we are not alone. Greater is he who live in you and me is greater than the one in the world.

Proverbs 3:5-6 (KJV) Trust in the Lord with all thine heart; and lean not unto thine own understanding. In all thy ways acknowledge him, and he shall direct thy path.

Being Humble In Heart
And In Spirit

Whoever heeds instruction is on the path to life, but he who rejects reproof leads others astray. Blessed is the pure in heart for they shall see the kingdom of God. Life is what God say it is, the commandment of our heavenly father; not the laws of man.

All of life is only a temporary arrangement, but where will you go after death? We need to humble ourselves before God. Furthermore, whether you are religious or simply do not believe in any religion; you still need to settle this most important question, because after a brief earth life man goes to his eternal destiny.

Ecclesiastes 12:5 (KJV) Also when they shall be afraid of that which is high, and fears shall be in the way, and the almond tree shall flourish, and the grasshopper shall be a burden, and desire shall fail: because man goeth to his long home, and the mourners go about the streets.

Ecclesiastes 12:7 (KJV) then shall the dust return to the earth as it was: and the spirit shall return unto God who gave it. Hebrews 9:27 (NIV) and just as each person is destined to die once and after that comes judgment.

Ecclesiastes 12:13-14 (NIV) But, my child, let me give you some further advice: Be careful, for writing books is endless, and much study wears you out. That is the whole story. Here now is my conclusion:

Fear God and obey his commands, for this is everyone's duty. God will judge us for everything we do, including every secret thing, whether good or bad.

You cannot hide from God. Proverbs 15:3 (KJV) The eyes of the Lord are in every place, beholding the evil and the good.

Corinthians 1:15-3 (KJV) For I delivered unto you first of all that which I also received, how that Christ died for our sins according to the scriptures.

Matthew 5:13 (NIV) You are the salt of the earth. But what good is salt if it has lost its flavor? Can you make it salty again? It will be thrown out and trampled underfoot as worthless.

Life is full of surprises anything can happen in a moment. Likewise, the earth is losing its flavor; after it had a sense and feeling of heaven. Moreover, it is the people in the world. Many of us have decided to trade our salt for something a little sweeter than the truth.

Moreover, all human beings have free will of choice and choices to make in all the things we do and say. Birds of a feather flock together; one thing I know and seen in this world, we all have to die at some point in time, death is a guarantee. It can knock at anyone's door at any time.

John 6:63 (NIV) The spirit alone gives eternal life. And the flesh accomplishes nothing. And the very words I have spoken to you are spirit and life.

The happier you become the more you see that nobody cares. Furthermore, when you become peaceful and have a relationship with God your relationship with people will change. If God is for you who can be against you, the ones that does not know him. When heaven came to earth, his own people did not believe him and knew him.

If my life is fruitless it does not matter who praise me, and if my life is fruitful, it does not matter who criticizes me. I know who love and care for me, my God of Jesus Christ. God is not something above humanity, God is something hidden within humanity.

Seek And You Will Find

Matthew 6:33-34 (NIV) Seek the kingdom God above all else, and live righteously, and he will give you everything you need. So don't worry about tomorrow, for tomorrow will bring its own worries. Today's trouble is enough for today.

The truth come by hearing the words of God, the truth come by being in silent, in the spirit and being humble before God. Speak the truth and the truth will set you free, whom Christ set free will be free indeed.

The truth comes by reading the words of God, hearing it and doing it. If you and I pay attention to what is happening in the world, you will get to see many people are turning away from the word of God, the truth and their faith in God.

I pray that God through our Lord Christ Jesus will shine his light for us and for those who are walking in darkness to see his way.

Many people are seeking the laws of man, furthermore looking to their own understanding. God write his laws and his commandments down for us to obey. Who have ears will hear what the spirit has to say.

God also sent his son to die for our sins. Respect God's word; proverb 13:13-16 (NIV) People who despise advice are asking for trouble; those who respect a command will succeed.

Jesus Christ commands us to seek God first with all, above all; Jesus said believe in him and in the one who send him. Furthermore, love one another as he loves you.

The instruction of the wise is like a life-giving fountain; those who accept it avoid the snares of death. A person with good sense is respect; a treacherous person is headed for destruction. Wise people think before they act; fools do not and even brag about their foolishness.

It seems like human kind is trying to recreate what God has created, they are not only trying now but from the beginning of time. Many of us are trying to be something we are not.

Why try to become something or someone; when we are already a masterpiece. God created us in his own image and likeness; why many of us are trying to recreate and change ourselves.

It is possible that we are saying we do not love ourselves, and the creator of us. If you and I do not love ourselves; then who will love us and how will we get love and feel love.

A person without love is like a body without the breath of life, hope, faith and with no action. A tree without roots; a river without water, a child without a father and a house without a roof.

A dead body does not feel or have any feeling; moreover, a dead body cannot move on its own. God created us from the dust therefore we are part of the earth; our body become one with nature when we die, our body return to the earth, ash to ash, dust to dust.

In addition, our spirit returns to God, to its maker and to its creator. God has given the believer of his son Jesus Christ the Holy Spirit of life, love, joy and peace.

However, it seem like many of us do not see and appreciate the richness and sacrifice that was given for our freedom. Furthermore, many of us become beggars, still looking and asking for more. Example a man's belly can only hold as much as it can hold until it is full.

Moreover, searching, man is seeking himself; he knows he is, but he does not know whom he is. Furthermore, he and she is seeking their own way, lost in their own selves. Your beautiful image; all glory and praise to you on high with honor and grace Lord Jesus.

Lord thank you for your wisdom and your understanding, through your Holy Spirit that lives in me with perfect love. Lord Jesus open up my understanding to your words to know you more in my spirit and heart within your care.

Lord continue to give me the strength to worship you in all that I do. Lord gravitate your faith, love, joy, peace, wisdom, understanding and let your Holy Spirit bring me closer to you.

Lord fill me with your spirit of strength, strengthen me Lord in my weakness so I may be strong in faith to overcome the tricks from the devil. Lord awaken my spirit within me to be awake of your blessing and will for my life; Lord Jesus fill me with your spirit of awareness to know who is from you and who is not.

Lord shine your light of love in me, over me, under me, above me and around me, through your Holy Spirit in the name of Christ Jesus I pray. Amen.

How You See You
Counterfeit Or Original

When God created the heavens and the earth, God saw everything he had created was good even you and me. Then something happened, human kind has disobeyed the creator instruction in what they should do and should not do.

Moreover, everything had changed after disobeying the creator of all things seen and unseen; by a make belief and counterfeit lie. Furthermore, the life for human kind became a blame game.

Then humankind was being exit, out of paradise to live in a counterfeit world. In the beginning, humankind had a choice and they did make that choice.

Moreover, we still have a choice to make, to live in paradise or a counterfeit world. Jesus the Christ said in his words, I am the way the truth and the life; no one can go to the father but only through me first. I put before you life and death, blessing and curse. Jesus also said that he has overcome the world and it is finish.

John 16:33 (NIV) I have told you all this so that you may have peace in me. Here on earth you will have many trials and sorrow, but take heart because I have overcome the world.

Romans 12:21(NIV) Don't let evil conquer you, but conquer evil by doing good. When we live in love, no matter what come our way, our heavenly father will be living in you and me, and you and me in him. God is love and love is God.

A Prayer To The Lord

Heavenly father I pray in the name of your son Jesus Christ and through your Holy Spirit. Lord cleanse me with the blood of Christ Jesus and free me from all darkness and unseen powers, so I may walk in your light.

Lord let your Holy Spirit guide me into your light of salvation, mercy, grace, love and truth. Lord fill and join your spirit of love, peace, joy, faith, and strengthen my spirit Lord. Father thank you for your love and faithfulness in all that you do and say. I love you because you first love me and showed me how to love, not only me but also others. In the name of Jesus Christ, I pray, Amen.

By Color Or Skin

We are one big family in the name of our lord, father and creator of Jesus Christ. We are many parts that comes together to make up one body in Christ. Furthermore, we are his kings and priest.

We may not look the same or alike, moreover we were all made in the image and likeness of God the creator of the heavens and the earth. However, in the world, we will go through suffering; just because of the color of our skin; the country we came from and the God of Jesus Christ we serve and believe in with love, hope, faith, and the courage to share that with one another.

Furthermore, we as human beings go through suffering in the same way. 1 Peter 4:12-13 (NIV) Dear friends, don't be surprised at the fiery trials you are going through, as if something strange were happening to you.

Instead, be very glad for these trials make you partners with Christ in his suffering, so that you will have the wonderful joy of seeing his glory when it is revealed to all the world.

Remember to seek God first above all that you may do, put your faith and trust in His son Jesus and help one another showing them love, affection and kindness. Moreover, never stop doing good and do not get tired of doing good.

1 Peter 5: 19 (NIV) So if you are suffering in a manner that please God, keep on doing what is right, and trust your lives to the God who created you, for he will never fail you.

God will not give us more than what we cannot handle; keep this in mind God made a promise through his son Jesus that he will never leave us nor forsaken us. He also promised us eternal life when we believe in the one he had sent into the world to pay the price for our sins. God is a God that does not lie; he is a just God, a God of his words in obedience.

1 Corinthians 10: 12-13 (NIV) If you think you are standing strong, be careful not to fall. The temptations in your life are no different from what others experience and God is faithful. He will not allow the temptation to be more than you can stand. When you are tempted, he will show you a way out so that you can endure.

We are all creatures created by our heavenly father, who loves us dearly. Furthermore, many of us know that we came into the world; therefore, we do not do the things of the world. A world divided and set up by the people of the world with a counterfeit race, religion, tradition and culture.

Moreover, do not judge and look at a person, by his or her color of their skin, look at the God who created everything. The creator is everywhere all we have to do is be grateful and acknowledge his presence when suffering and at all times good as well as not so good times.

We are all in the valley of the shadow of death, trying to get to the mountain. Indeed if we have eyes to see the mountain then we may have an idea; that the one on the mountain can see us and will help us get there safe. Lastly do not judge the book by its cover, discover what is hidden in it.

A Prayer To The Lord

Heavenly father of our Lord Jesus Christ thank you for the breath of life; I thank you with the feeling of a grateful heart and spirit you have created within me. I love you with the love you gave me, and your love you have shown and share with me through your son Jesus Christ.

Lord, you are all I needed and wanted; Lord, I see nothing in this man made world that could give me that peace, joy, comfort, love, faith, hope, understanding, wisdom, courage and strength. Only you Lord can give me that blessing and eternal life.

Lord I can see the love you have for your children and the love you have for the one who are lost and broken. Lord all my heart can say is thank you, because your love is all I need. Lord your love never fails, it never gives up and it never runs out on me.

Lord you complete me in ways I cannot explain. Lord, you know my heart because you created it within my inner part. Lord I cannot change to be what I want to be, but only what you want me to be. Lord I will suffer for you, before I suffer for the things in the world that will give me a temporary joy. Father God I pray that you will keep me on the original path to you; protect me from the counterfeit light, fill me with your light. Lord Jesus shine your light for my feet.

Heavenly father I ask you in the name of Jesus Christ for the strength to lose the world that was created in me when I enter in to a world of sin. Therefore, I can find myself in you and in your unfailing love, grace, faithfulness and your kindness.

Lord wash me as you wash your disciples feet; Lord cleanse me and sanctify my spirit within me with your glorious light, presence and your blood. Therefore, I may walk in the path you have made for me.

Lord widen and deepen my heart and spirit within me with love and let your love flow in me like a river of living water. Lord so I may learn to be possessed by your love and to rise above myself, strong in ecstasy, love and bliss in the name of Jesus Christ I pray. Amen.

Ephesians 6:19 (NIV) And pray for me, too. Ask God to give me the right words so I can boldly explain God's mysterious plan that the Good News is for Jew and Gentiles alike.

Romans 8:16 (KJV) The Spirit itself beareth witness with our spirit, that we are children the of God. Therefore, fear cannot save us in poverty and unbelieves. It is in being courageous, believing, and having faith and putting your trust, hope and faith in God the father and his son Jesus the Christ.

In love Lord, you have punished yourself on the cross for our sins; you have given us your name as a shield of protection in the world.

We were living in a world without a father and you came to set us free; by setting an example in showing your love for all.

Therefore, we can do the same with each other, likewise sacrificing one for all with a feeling I cannot explain. However, with a hope, a faith and a trust in my Lord and savior Jesus Christ. Lord you never push or force me to come to you. I saw the door and I felt the presence of your comfort, peace, joy and love in my heart, body, spirit and soul with a voice saying you are not alone you belong to me.

I did not know what the meaning of fear is; I only had an idea of the word. When I enter into a world of words, than fear came about, fear presents itself. It was not a fear of the world I felt, it was the fear of the one who created the world. The beginning of wisdom is the fear of God.

Number 6:24-26 (KJV) The Lord bless thee, and keep thee. The Lord make his face shine upon thee, and be gracious unto thee. The Lord lift up his countenance upon thee, and give thee peace.

The Man

This is a poem of the man. When a man and a person do something wrong, many of the time, they are aware of it and they still do it. The world we are living in is beautiful it just have shady, selfish and wicked people in it who only think about themselves.

When evil and wicked people do wrong things, they have people to cover up for them. Remember the Lord sees all things and he knows what is in a person heart. Moreover, many may not see and know what we are doing and thinking, but God knows everything.

Therefore whatever a person thinks in his or her heart so they will be. A seed is sow, it will become a tree and whatever tree it becomes, he or she will eat it fruit.

Moreover, happiness comes through the suffering of another person pain; furthermore, that is what many people feed off to feel good of them self.

A rich person shines for a while, but a person with the love of God shines forever. A man with a lot of money have many friends until his money runs out on him; and so will his so call friends will run out and run away from him too.

A person wants what they do not have and a person do not like what they have. Grateful people never complain but give thanks even when they do not have anything.

Many of us want to win the war but not many of us has been in the war or the battlefield. However, Jesus did win the war therefore, we can be free.

Romans 8:15 (NIV) So have not receive the spirit that makes you fearful slaves. Instead, you receive God's spirit when he adopted you as him own children. Now we call him, sons, Abba father.

Love Is The Way

Love is not just a word. Love is the spirit of the creator of all things seen and unseen. Love is Jesus Christ. Love is an everlasting feeling. Love is a light that shines the way for us to see.

Love is the way. Love is everything. Love is everywhere. Love covers all transgression. Love is the truth and the light.

Love is the way. Love is special. Love is in every hearts. Love is beautiful. Love is in the air. Love has no fear. Love is the start and the end.

Love is the way. Love is the joy of our strength. Love is a mile in every smile. Love is a river that never stops flowing. Love is the way. Love is like raindrops that fall, all we have to do is allow it to touch us. Love lives forever. Love never dies.

Love is the way. Love is pure and kind. Love is patience and time. Love is a blessing that will always shines. Love is you and I. Love is the one who created you and me.

Love is the way. Love is the cycle of life. Love is happiness. Love is hope and faith. Love is understanding. Love is compassion. Love is the wind that blows. Love is the breath you take.

Love is the way. Love is the presence of the most high. Love is amazing. Love is inner peace. Love is the heart, Spirt and soul. Love is the blood in our veins.

Love is the way. Love is not a belief. Love is knowing. Love is action. Love is loving oneself. Love is number one. Love is a light in every hearts. Love is freedom. Love is all in one.

Love is the way. Love is the root in our heart. Love is the centre and soul of our heart and spirit. Love is a form of energy. Love is a spirit you cannot see, but you can feel its energy. Love lives within you and me.

Love is not something, which can become Love; it is what it is. Love is God, and God is love, whoever lives in love, lives in God and God in them. If you have everything and you do not have love, you have nothing. It's like having a tree without roots. Jesus is love.

Being An Original As You Are

God made man and woman in his own image and likeness; therefore we were all created by the original hands of our heavenly father of our Lord Jesus Christ.

Moreover, many of us have try so hard to change who we are into whom we are not, furthermore this has been going on for such a long time. Humankind is still trying to find who they are.

When you are original, you should stay original, do not conform to the things in the world and loose that beauty. Many generations has passed down their culture and theory of how you should live and who you should be. The beauty of life is being who God created you to be. Remember God created you and me in his image and likeness; therefore, his beauty within us can shine his love through us for all to see.

In the beginning, God gave Adam the dominion over all the world. Adam yielded dominion to Satan, who then became the God of the world.

Now the power and dominion was renew for us to rule and be free, because of the power that Christ has given to you and me; No one can take it away again, in deceiving or trading the original to be something different than the truth.

Our Lord Christ Jesus had conquered death and the grave, all power of darkness and death was broken. Furthermore, we have direct access to God the father through Christ Jesus.

2 Corinthians 5:17 (KJV) Therefore if any man be in Christ, he is a new creature: old things are passed away; behold, all things are became new.

Ephesians 2:17-18 (NIV) He brought this Good News of peace to you Gentiles who were far away from him, and peace to the Jew who were near. Now all of us can come to the father through the same Holy Spirit because of what Christ has done for us.

We have been rescued from the domain of darkness; Colossians 1:13 (NIV) For he has rescued us from the kingdom of darkness and transferred us into the kingdom of his dear son.

Proverbs 21: 21 (NIV) Whoever pursues righteousness and unfailing love, righteousness, and honor.

A Prayer To Our Heavenly Father

Our father who art in heaven, blessed be you Holy name thank you for the breath of life. Thank you Lord for creating me in your own likeness, image and in your love. I thank you Lord for this day and every breath I take in saying thank you. I love you Lord with the love you have filled my heart, spirit and soul with.

Father God I thank you for life, for health and the voice to say thank you. Lord without you I cannot do anything on my own, your presence has filled me with peace and your joy has given me strength.

Thank you Lord for making a way for me, when there seem to be no way; Lord you are the way the truth and the light for me to see. So many times, Lord you have forgiven me and made a way for me in your love, kindness and mercy in the name of Jesus Christ, I thank you, Amen.

Father God in the name of your son, our Lord Jesus Christ I ask you to renew the inner man in me to see the things that is eternal. Lord Jesus open the eyes of my heart I want to see you;

Lord Jesus open my ears I want to hear you; Lord Jesus open my heart and fill it with your love, your strength, your courage, your wisdom, your understanding, your Grace, your faith, your hope, your mercy, your forgiveness, your peace, your blood, and the power of your Holy Spirit to do your will in the name of Jesus.

Lord Jesus I need you more than ever, you are my source of strength and joy. In your presence, Lord there is peace, love and joy, walk with me Lord Jesus and shine your light for me to see victory in the seed you planted into my heart where your Holy Spirit lives.

Lord cover my loved ones and me with the blood of Jesus Christ and anoint our head and hearts with your hands of protection. Lord you are beautiful beyond description, your love have a feeling inside of me I cannot express with words; but with your spirit of truth. Lord it is a feeling beyond my imagination.

Lord Jesus guide and fill me with the strength and power of your Holy Spirit to walk by faith and not by sight. Lord draw me close to you, clothed me with love, with light, with forgivingness, and the with blood of Jesus Christ; Lord Jesus cover me with your presence of joy, peace, love and truth. Lord Jesus when you say yes no one can say no.

Lord Jesus where your Holy Spirt is there is freedom. Thank you Lord for your love, the cross and the price you have paid for me, thank you for your stripes, because of your stripes I am heal. Lamb of God you are worthy, in your name all glory, honor, worship and praise is your now and forever. In the name of Jesus Christ I pray, thank you Lord. Amen.

Blessing For Obedience

Deuteronomy 28:1-2 (NIV) If you fully obey the Lord your God, and carefully keep all his commandments that I am giving you today, the Lord your God will set you high above all the nations of the world.

You will experience all these blessing if you obey the Lord your God.

Proverbs 13:21 (NIV) Trouble chases sinners, while blessing reward the righteous.

A prayer

Lead Me to the Rock

Psalm 61:1-8 (NIV) O God, listen to my cry! Hear my prayer! From the ends of the earth, I cry to you for help when my heart is overwhelmed. Lead me to the towering rock of safety, for you are my safe refuge, a fortress where my enemies cannot reach me. Let me live forever in your sanctuary, safe beneath the shelter of your wings.

A Lover For The Things Above Or A Lover For The Things In The World

Numbers 6:24-26 (NIV) The Lord bless thee, and keep thee. The Lord make his face to shine upon thee, and be gracious unto thee. The Lord lift up his countenance upon the, and give thee peace. The good Lord gives and takes he is a just God; he made everything with love and he had to send his only son to show us what true love is.

Many of us say that we love and have love. What kind of love are you talking about? That is an awakening question; there is two kind of love that is my opinion on that topic. Everyone is entitled to his or her own opinions.

What is love? God is love, love is not one own understanding, love is far more than the understanding of our human mind. Love is God the father of our Lord Jesus Christ. Moreover, laying down one life for another; that is true love, loving someone is not love, if it does not come from the heart within you, then it may be a form of infatuation for the flesh. Likewise, loving someone with the love from our Lord is a true blessing of love.

The love of the world is a form of infatuation; the love of the world is an enemy to God. Furthermore, love for something is not really, or what it may seem to be. The eyes will see what it wants to see, but the heart knows the beauty of it all.

Moreover, many of us will say we do not love this person or that person, but we love God, how can that be, when a person loves someone, they cannot see and do not love the one they can see. God's word say you are a liar, how can you love one you cannot see and do not love the one you do see.

God is love and who ever lives in love lives in God and God lives in them. If you say you love God and hate your brother and sister you are a liar and the truth in not in you. We should not say we hate or don't love a person, what I think we should say is we do not like what the person is doing or done.

Moreover, many of us have love for money more than we have love for God, ourselves and one another. Example the love for money is the root of all evil; I am not saying you cannot have money. I am just saying be content with what you have. The Lord knows what you need. Beware! Guard against every kind of greed. Life is not measured by how much you own. Lastly look at the birds and the tree they do not reap or sow but God take care of them; what make you think that he will not take care of you too.

We are all running a race in the world, many of us are like rabbits and many of us are like turtles; moreover, trying to win a race in competing against each other.

Luke 12:21 (NIV) Yes, a person is a fool to store up earthly wealth but not have a rich relationship with God.

Luke 12:32-34 (NIV) So don't be afraid, little flock. For it gives your father great happiness to give you the kingdom.

Sell your possessions and give to those in need. This will store up treasure for you in heaven! And the purses of heaven never get old or develop holes. Your treasure will be safe; no thief can steal it and no moth can destroy it. Wherever your treasure is, there the desire of your heart will also be.

A Prayer To The Lord

Our father who are in heaven, thank you for all that you have and still doing in my life. Thank you for the greatest treasure you have given me with your love.

Thank you for opening the eyes of my heart to see and feel you Lord. Thank you father for your Holy Spirit of power, love, light, faith, peace, joy, comfort, health, strength, hope, protection, guidance, grace, salvation and everlasting life in your son Jesus Christ.

Lord continue to guide me into your light of truth, glory and grace. Lord bind the power of every darkness and evil Spirits that may try to come in and around me in the name of Jesus Christ I pray.

Lord make your face shine on me with your love, joy and peace within my soul. Thank you Lord for your final words it is finish. My future is in your hands; all my fear is gone because you live within my Spirit father God.

Lord let every beat of my heart feel your love, peace, joy, comfort; furthermore, let my heart beat the wave of your sweet melody of love for all to hear.

Therefore, I may be awake in every moment of your presence. Father God let the words that come from my heart let it be your words. Lord let the words I speak be your words not mine.

Lord in my up and down, in sickness and in health, in sadness and joy, in whatever I may go through and encounter; I will rejoice, give thanks, praise and worship you.

Father God you made everything; I am not my own, I belong to you. Lord I pray that you will receive my Spirit when I leave this world, in the name of your son Jesus Christ I pray heavenly father, Amen.

The Desires Of Selfishness Will Fail

In life, everyone have some kind of desires; Likewise, a desire to be or to become something. Moreover, everyone is the author of his and her life. However, God is the author of everything. Likewise, everyone has a story to tell.

Furthermore, the story of all times has been told already with a choice of free will and love, until the finisher return to separate the sheep from the goats.

The world we are living in is a world of self-desires, needs and wants. A life of give me, give me; the eyes see, the eyes want. The desires of selfishness become more aware in the heart of this generation. To illustrate a little more, man's life on earth is warfare of testing of their faith.

Ephesians 6:11:12 (KJV) Put on the whole armour of God, that ye may be able to stand against the wiles of the devil. For we wrestle not against flesh and blood, but against principalities, against powers, against the rulers of the darkness of this world, against spiritual wickedness in high places.

2 Corinthians 10:3-4 (KJV) For though we walk in the flesh, we do not war after the flesh. For the weapons of our warfare are not carnal, but mighty through God to the pulling down of strong holds.

Acts 20:24 (NIV) But my life is worth nothing to me unless I use it for finishing the work assigned me by the Lord Jesus- the work of telling others the Good News about the wonderful grace of God.

Philippians 3:14 (KJV) I press toward the mark for the prize of the high calling of God in Christ Jesus. The desire of a person heart is where their treasure will be. Luke 12:34 (NIV) wherever your treasure is, there the desire of your heart will also be.

Luke 12:15 (NIV) Then he said, Beware! Guard against every kind of greed. Life is not measured by how much you own.

The devil will try the same trick on us. The same tricks Satan try with Jesus when he told Jesus he would give him the whole world if he bow down and worship him.

Luke 4:5-8 (NIV) Then the devil took him up and revealed to him all the kingdoms of the world in a moment of time. I will give you the glory of these kingdoms and authority over them," the devil said, because they are mine to give to anyone I please. I will give it to you if you will worship me. Jesus replied, the scriptures say, you must worship the Lord your God and serve only him.

Resist the devil and he will flee. Psalm 62:7-10 (NIV) My victory and honor come from God alone. He is my refuge, a rock where no enemy can reach me. O my people, trust in him at all time. Pour out your heart to him, for God is our refuge. Common people are worthless as a puff of wind, and the powerful are not what they appear to be. If you weigh them on the scales, together they are lighter than a breath of air.

Don't make your living by extortion or put your hope in stealing. And if your wealth increases, don't make it the center of your life.

The devil is a form of light but he is full of darkness and tricks. He can disguise himself to the fake version, because he is not an original; and he knows that he has no power over you and me. That is why he will try to deceive us with his false representation of language, worldly things and counterfeit lies and light.

John 10:10 (NIV) The thief's purpose is to steal and kill and destroy. My purpose is to give them a rich and satisfying life. The devil will promise gifts to many people, but does not give it; he is like clouds and wind that bring no rain.

James 3:16 (NIV) For wherever there is jealousy and selfish ambition, there you will find disorder and evil of every kind.

Romans 12:2 (NIV) Don't copy the behavior and customs of this world, but let God transform you into a new person by changing the way you think. Then you will learn to know God's will for you, which is good and pleasing and perfect.

Proverbs 16:33 (NIV) We may throw the dice, but the Lord determines how they fall. Lastly be aware because the devil is roaming the earth to see whom he can devour.

A Prayer For Spiritual Growth

Ephesians 3:14-21 (NIV) When I think of all this, I fall to my knees and pray to the father, the creator of everything in heaven and on earth. I pray that from his glorious, unlimited resources he empower you with inner strength through his spirit. Then Christ will make his home in your hearts as you trust in him. Your roots will grow down into God's love and keep you strong.

And may you have the power to understand, as all God's people should, how wide, how long, how high, and how deep his love is. May you experience the love of Christ, though it is too great to understand fully. Then you will be made complete with all the fullness of life and power that comes from God.

Now all glory to God, who is able, through his mighty power at work within us, to accomplish infinitely more we might ask or think. Glory to him in the Church and in Christ Jesus through all generations forever and ever! Amen.

Do Not Bite The Hand
That Feeds You

In the life that we are living in now; likewise in this time and age of this generation. Moreover, things seem to be getting challenging and tough for many of us as time goes by.

Furthermore, the more we become aware and see the things that are happening in the world today. The more many of us become afraid and think that we are alone in this. Moreover, many will question where God is, even question if there is a God and where is he.

Every time and many of the times, when we see things happening; that may seem to be, beyond our control. We start to question and complain, Instead of praying.

Although from time to time God hears the prayers of anyone who sincerely cries out to him in time of need, he is not bound by his word to do this. That is why men and women are sickened by the horrors, rumors and demands of war.

Isaiah 59:1-2 (NIV) Behold, the Lords hand is not shortened, that it cannot save; neither his ear heavy, that it cannot hear; but your iniquities have separated between you and your God, and your sins have hid his face from you, that he will not hear.

Jesus said do not let your heart be trouble for these things will happen, take to heart I will be with you on till the end of the age; to illustrate more from Jesus words, Jesus said I will never leave you are forsaken you.

It seems like the love for one another is getting colder every day. Moreover, many are losing their faith in God and turning to the world. In addition, many are looking out for his and her own self; trying so hard to do whatever it takes, to get wherever they think they need to be.

Remember not all roads will lead you to where you think you are going. Every day we bite the hand that feeds us; just by the way we think, the way we act, the things we do and say; lastly the way we respond to the situation.

Jesus said that he is the way the truth and the life, no one come to the father but by him first. If you look closely, you will see the birds and the trees they do not reap or sow but the creator of the heaven and the earth feeds and take care of them. What make you think that he will not take care of us when we ask him?

Moreover, look at the birds and trees they do not talk and complain like we do; they seems to be enjoying what the creator is doing for them. Furthermore, they seem to be more grateful than many of us.

So stop biting the hand that feeds you and let us be more grateful; and start putting our faith, trust and everything in the hands of God.

Likewise, many people I have encountered with will say. That is human's nature to complain; my reply is why, we as human beings cannot be more grateful for what we have than what we do not have.

I think because many of us only see self in the mirror; remember our body was made from many parts. Jesus Christ did not see himself he saw every one of us; Christ did not come to be served but to serve.

When hard times come to you, do not run to the mountain, run to the one who made the mountain, he is bigger than the mountain.

Look to the one who say come to me all who have heavy burden and are weary with heavy leaden; furthermore, look to him, who was and is to come; his name is Jesus Christ.

The story of David and goliath, David did not run away from Goliath he run to his God, and put his faith and trust in him, because he knew his God is bigger than everything, he knew who is with him; and what who was with him can do. Moreover, go to the hand that feeds you and me not bite it.

The fishes and bread that were feed to the people who came to Jesus; it was enough for five thousand; I think it will be enough for all who are hungry with a grateful and sincere heart. Jesus said ask for anything in his name and it shall be given to you.

It can be easy to be unthankful and ungrateful, than to be thankful and grateful. Because when many of us ask for something and we do not get it. I think many of us know exactly what we are doing and asking for; saying it does not mean it. Your motives have to be right when asking.

Moreover, one of the biggest issues in many of our life is when we ask for something and we do not get it; the reason behind that could be our motive is wrong, or it may have nothing to do with the will of God for our lives.

Likewise, we see what others have and we want the same thing. Moreover, everything may look good and beautiful on the outside, but the inside could be dead. Lastly a tomb on the outside look beautiful, but the question is, what is on the inside the tomb, dead bones.

Furthermore, we may not have any idea to how people get what we see them with or what they do to get it. Moreover, we always find a way to bite the hand that feed us. That is why when a man and a woman plant a seed; God is the one that make it grow, he is the one that bless everything.

If we know how to give our children good gifts and the things when they ask for them; what is stopping you and me from asking our heavenly father.

Luke 11:13 (KJV) If ye then, being evil, know how to give good gifts to your children; how much more shall your heavenly father give the Holy Spirit to them that ask him? There is an old saying you only miss the water when the well runs dry.

We are satisfied in God; proverbs 13: 25) (KJV) The righteous eateth to the satisfying of his soul; but the belly of the wicked shall want. However, the word of God grew and multiplied. Seek him first above all for all your wants and your needs. God is the head of all things seen and unseen.

The Divine Love

The source of the divine love has fallen upon me, entering into my heart and spirit, like the cool breeze from the ocean of unfailing love;

Filling me with joy, love and peace, I felt myself floating into the arms of the sky; where I saw the beauty of the earth and the light from the heavens surrounding it.

The wings of the Lord presence was holding me up as I soar through the clouds like an eagle; Feeling the source of comfort, love and peace. A feeling that never ends, but only repeat itself with divine love.

The power from the Lord love has captured my soul. I was found and never to be lost, or to be out of his sight again.

Furthermore, from the shadows of the world and the darkness that is in it. The Lord has showed me the way and I had followed it with the free will and choice that he had given me.

My soul rejoices with a never-ending joy and peace; I am protected and blessed in the name of the Lord Jesus Christ.

In his promises and love for me, I can do all things through Christ Jesus who strengthens me. The divine love from God will never fail you and me nor will he leave us. All we have to do is welcome him back into our lives, by opening the door to our hearts.

Jesus said I am at the door of your heart; when you hear the knock and invite me in, I will come in and dine with you. This is a poem of Divine love in the name of Jesus.

A Prayer For One Another

Heavenly father thank you for your blessing, guidance and love for all of your creation. Heavenly father I pray for the strength to continue in helping and sharing your blessing with one another in the name of Jesus Christ.

Lord fill me with your light and compassion of love to share it with those who are in need. Heavenly father I pray that you will strengthen me in my faith in you, so it may not fail me in doing what I have to do on my journey in this life.

Father God let your blessing of light and understanding bring all of your creation to become children to your love Lord.

I pray in the mighty name of Jesus Christ that we will all be filled with the wisdom and love from your Holy Spirit to be instrument for one another with love and comfort.

Father God shine your light through others and me so we may see not only our self; but others in us and you in others and in me. Lord let your joy be our strength in all the things that we do and say.

Father God let you wisdom from your Holy Spirit be our guide and the source to all our problems; Lord your presence gives me joy, love, boldness and peace to share with others. In Jesus name I pray Amen.

A Slave To What You Obey
And Self-Denial To The Truth

We are all slaves to something, someone or the things we chose to believe and follow. Many of us are living in self-denial. Moreover a bunch of know it all, outward but far from the truth inward.

In life, there is a lesson to learn; those lessons is learn to listen and listen to learn. The choice we have is to choose wisely, life or death, good judgement or bad judgement. The word of God said I put before you, life and death, blessing and curse choose life.

A seed is all we have to sow, therefore for it to become the result for the sower to receive the harvest. Example, the weatherman on the news, said there is strong wind and rain outside with great floods. Therefore, whoever is inside their house, he or she should stay inside.

Many of us will see an apple and still say it is a pear or a mango. Likewise, we deceive ourselves in manipulating others in believing; in what we want them to believe and not what they see.

To illustrate a little more, many of us not only live in self-denial and deceive ourselves; we also deceive our children, by telling them that Santa Claus and the tooth fairy is real. The list can go on as long as you want it too. Moreover, many of you know what I am talking about, speak the truth, tell the truth and live the truth, because everything we are sowing is a seed. In addition, we all have to give account for it all.

A Prayer To The Lord

Heavenly father thank you for all that you are still doing in the lives of others and in me. My heart is so grateful and full of your love, joy and light. Lord you are the light of my life.

Lord thank you for showing me the way to your everlasting promise; Lord you are all I have. Lord, you have never failed me, but everything and everyone did.

Lord I ask for your strength, the whole shield of Amor protection to protect me as I go through my every day; in love, comfort, peace and your guidance, in the name of Jesus Christ.

Father God I pray for the wisdom, the understanding, the strength, the knowledge and the love to diligently seek you; to be in obedience in your will, words and love for one another in my life.

Heavenly father through Jesus Christ and your Holy Spirit increase within me with spiritual growth, strength, love, forgiveness, joy, happiness, hope, peace, faith and confidence in God our father.

Father God remove all doubt, unbelief in my heart and mind. Fill my mind, heart, Spirit and soul to stay faithful and focus not on my will but your will.

Father God I believe that you are the rewarder. I put my faith and trust in the name of your son Jesus Christ my redeemer. Father God I know without real faith it is impossible to please you.

Lord fill my Spirit to your understanding and repentance in your blessed name, to be cleanse and to stay Holy. Father God you are the treasure in my heart and soul. The living waters that purify within my heart, body, mind, Spirit and soul; with your blood Lord Jesus as I kneel at the foot of the cross. In Jesus Christ name, I pray and call upon. Amen.

Who Or What Is Influencing You

We are living in a divided world where we have the choices to make and take. The road that leads to life and death; moreover, everything is divided in to two. Therefore, we all have free will and a choice to make; every day that God our heavenly father has blessed us with. That is why, when we pray. We have to ask our heavenly father to give us this day our daily bread.

The influence of many things that is happening in our lives today has to do with the choices we make, the things we say, the things we do, and the choices we let others make for us. Furthermore, it may also have to do with our ancestor and past generation, likewise the choices they had made.

Jesus is the way to everyone's problems; he is the word that became flesh the light of the world. In the beginning, he was and is.

Wherever, we sow a seed it will grow and whom you hang around, will show too what is influencing you. Likewise, the instrument that God use through others will shine the light of Christ on you.

Take time to listen; Proverbs 18:2 (NIV) Fool have no interest understanding; they only want to air their own opinion.

Wisdom speaks for itself; proverbs 15:2 (KIV) The tongue of the wise useth knowledge aright; but the mouths of fools poureth out foolishness.

The words that come out of our mouths are what influencing us; the power of words, will build you and me, and it will destroy us at the same time.

Moreover, the things we are watching on the television and the music we are listening to have a big influence in our lives. Example, ears, eyes and mouth.

The Power Of Words

Matthew 15:18 (NIV) But the words you speak come from the heart-that is what defiles you.

Words are powerful, in many ways. The power of words lives in the tongue; it is life and death. The power of words can make and break you.

The power of words and love Lives in the heart; the power of words brings hope and faith. The power of words can bring and take.

The power of words enters into my heart as a shield of faith. The power of words comes from within, using the power of love to help; not only ourselves, but others too.

The power of words sailing everywhere; do not let the power of words take over your life, but let it build you up and strengthen you with the words of God.

The power of words are a live wire, therefore you should use it wisely, because some day we will all have to give God account for every words that we sow.

Matthew 12:36 (NIV) And I tell you this, you must give an account on judgment day for every idle word you speak.

Ephesians 4:29 (NIV) Don't use foul or abusive language. Let everything you say be good and helpful, so that your words will be an encouragement to those who hear them.

Prayer To The Lord

Lord Jesus Christ, shepherd of all souls, who called the apostles to be fishers of men, rise up new apostles in your Holy Church. Teach us to serve you and to reign with you, possess us to possess all the things you created.

Kindle in the young hearts of your sons and daughters the fire of zeal for our souls. Make us eager to spread your kingdom upon earth, Grant us the courage to follow you.

Who are the way the truth and the life; that lives reigns forever and ever in the name of Jesus Christ I pray, Amen.

Breaking The Cycle

1 John 1:9 (NIV) But if we confess our sins, he is faithful and just to forgive us our sins and to cleanse us from all wickedness.

Before entering into this world our freedom has been giving to us, with the responsibility of who we should be and what we should do. Furthermore, entering into a world of words, born into a world; where and when the choices been made for us by others.

Moreover, writing in everyone's head and mind, what he or she is going to be, where he or she is going to be born and so the list goes on and on, even when we die.

I see that everybody has the answers for everyone questions; but it seems like they do not even know the answer for their own questions and problems. We are all prisoners of ourselves and prisoners of who are in control of us; moreover, we are slave to them.

Likewise, to be a slave you and I have to think like a slave; and to be free you and I have to think like a free person, he and she.

Likewise, inexperienced an innocent child, who lacks knowledge of being; the principle is that one is innocent until proven guilty.

Many will say yes, many will say no. there is a saying, do we really practice what we preach. All of us as living beings are been judge and been labeled already before getting a chance in this world, especially the children and believer of our Lord Jesus. So when you hear the saying innocent until proven guilty.

Example- a book is being judged before it is opened and has been looked in to; to see what is there inside of it. Likewise, judged by its cover.

Moreover, even looking into a book, we are still going to pass judgement. Furthermore, whether we are guilty or not. God is the judge.

Indeed, parents have a vital role in educating their children, not just by what they say, but what they say and what they do. The most important thing is in shaping a child's mind with words an example of what we say and do.

Jesus teaches us as parents how to grow up a child, putting in them while they are young the words of God; so when they get older they will not depart from them.

Proverbs 22:6 (NIV) Direct your children onto the right path, and when they are older, they will not leave it.

If we have not laid a Godly foundation for our children when they are small, it becomes all the more difficult to establish that foundation. When they mature into their teen years. There is an old saying bend the tree when it is young.

Proverbs 22:15 (NIV) A youngster's heart is filled with foolishness, but physical discipline will drive it far away. Proverbs 13:24 (NIV) Those who spare the rod of discipline hate their children. Those who love their children care enough to discipline them.

Ephesian 6:1-4 (NIV) Children, obey your parents because you belong to the Lord, for this is the right thing to do. Honor your father and mother. This is the first commandment with a promise. If you honor your father and your mother, things will go well for you, and you will have a long life on the earth.

Father, do not provoke your children to anger by the way you treat them. Rather, bring them up with discipline and instruction that comes from the Lord.

In the world today, most parents lack the wisdom and understanding on how to bring up a child. It seems most lately that the new age children of today are becoming the parents of their parents. Because they are telling their parents what to do, instead of the parent being the parent and not the other way around.

James 1:5-6 (NIV) If you need wisdom, ask our generous God, and he will give it to you. He will not rebuke you for asking. But when you ask him, be sure that your faith is in God alone. Do not waver, for a person with divided loyalty is as unsettled as a wave of the sea that is blown and tossed by the wind.

Our human nature-and the world around us- teaches a very contrary principle.

1 John 4:4 (KJV) Ye are of God, little children, and have overcome them; because greater is he that is in you, than he that is in the world.

1 John 5:4 (KJV) For whatsoever is born of God overcometh the world: and this is the victory that overcometh the world, even our faith.

A Prayer For Freedom

Our heavenly father of our Lord Jesus Christ, thank you for creating me in your own image and likeness; thank you for all that you have done and are still doing in my life today. Thank you for the awareness of your love and the relationship that you blessed me to have with you.

Father God I pray in the name of Jesus Christ not for you to take me out of the world, but to protect others and me from the evil one.

Lord Jesus I pray for the strength to do what you have called me to do and to stay rich in an intimate relationship with you; Lord I seek you first as you give me the strength, day by day to do everything that I have to do in your will for me.

Lord and my God, let your will be done, not mine but your will.

Father God I come to you my heavenly father for your grace, salvation, and guidance in your words of wisdom, understanding, strength and the awareness in your teaching of obedience and love.

Father God I give myself a way to you; the self that has been created by the parenting of the world. Lord Jesus I give myself a way to find myself in you. Lord Jesus you are the way the truth and the light for my eyes, my heart and feet to follow.

Lord continue to guide me on my journey as the salt and light of the world, therefore others may see your light shining through me.

Lord cover me with your protection and fill me with your Holy Spirit; Lord Jesus put your hedge of protection, mark and seal on me so that no evil in this world can affect and touch me. This I pray and ask in the name of Jesus Christ, to be transformed into your light, love and glory. Amen

The Person In The Mirror

James 1:22-25 (NIV) But don't just listen to God's word. You must do what it says. Otherwise, you are only fooling yourselves. For if you listen to the word and don't obey, it is like glancing at your face in a mirror.

You see yourself, walk away, and forget what you look like. But if you look carefully into the perfect law that sets you free, and if you do what it says and don't forget what you heard, then God will bless you for doing it.

and not hearers only, deceiving yourselves. For if anyone is a hearer of the word and not a doer, he is like a man who looks intently at his natural face in a mirror.

For he looks at himself and goes away and at once forgets what he was like. But the one who looks into the perfect law, the law of liberty, and perseveres, being no hearer who forgets but a doer who acts, he will be blessed in his doing.

King Solomon said, it is better to desire the things we have, than to have the things we desire. When we start with the person in the mirror, we will get to see what we do not want to become. When we make that change first in our lives, everything around us will change.

When we choose to walk into other people's shadow, we become a shadow of something we are not. Moreover, we come into a state of seeing not the truth. Furthermore, we start to live our lives in a state of denial, now self-denial becomes our image of who we are not.

The image of someone becoming something they are not; it is like catching water in a basket. Likewise, many of us do not want to be, but we like to become what we see and what others tell us we should be.

The devil is a liar and a thief; he is roaming the earth to seek whom he can devour. The devil comes to kill, steal and destroy anyone he can get a hold on, especially the believers of our Lord Jesus Christ.

Indeed, any person, he or she that wants to become something they are not is asking and looking for trouble. The devil is a thief and a lair, all he wants to do is to control our mind. He will try to steal our identity and give us an idea of what he wants us to be. The devil want to keep us away from the plan God has for us. Example-a mother will give birth to a baby. In addition, the mouth of a person gives birth to whatever he or she says and follows.

A tree will bear its fruits from the tree it comes from; you will know a tree by its fruit. If you are an apple tree that is what you are, so stop fooling yourselves into thinking that you are a pear tree, and that you could become a pear tree.

However, you can become a family tree in Gods family through Jesus Christ. We can do all things through Christ Jesus who strengthens you and me.

Example- an apple tree is an apple tree.

Many of us are still living in Egypt with Pharaoh. However, onto this present day many of us are still refusing to let go of Egypt and continue to the promise land. In addition leaving who we are not and being who we were created to be. Moreover, many of us chose to die a slave than to be free.

Many of us have left Egypt, and because many of us have left Egypt that does not mean we are free from Egypt. Likewise, many of us are still carrying Egypt within us. Lastly, you can take a person out of a place but you cannot take the place out of that person.

The only one that can take a person out off a place and a place out off a person is our Lord Jesus. He is the way the truth and the life; Jesus is the only way; remember whom the son of God set free is free indeed.

Life does not depend on how much you have, but how you enjoy life; how you live it and whom you are living it for. Likewise, there is a saying your action speaks so loud, I can hear what you are saying.

Indeed, we say that we do not care what other people may say about us. I will say really, if we say that we do not care that much, then why does what people say, about us have an effect on us. We repeat to others what has been told to us.

Likewise, we should let the truth set us free and not the lies of what others have to say about us.

The truth hurts and lies hurts as well; indeed the truth is what can and will set us free. The words of God is the truth and Jesus is the way the truth and the life.

We are all houses therefore you and me should know what is in our houses (the body- temple) that God has given us, and where Christ Holy Spirit lives.

I have to say many of us have traded our righteousness, image and faith in God, for the things in and from the world. I see through suffering many people find who they are, and what God wants us to see through our suffering.

There is a saying they will give you more to receive you less, and they will give you less to receive more.

I am free of condemnation (Romans 8:1) So now there is no condemnation for those who are in Christ Jesus. For those who walk not after the flesh, but after the Spirit.

Life is like a scale, which has two sides and a center, where we need to find it balance. Moreover, life is a blessing from our heavenly father of all creation; the father of our Lord Jesus Christ.

In this new age world, that been created for us to see not the way of God, but the way of the one that is of the world. Many of us see ourselves in many different ways, but there is a way we should see ourselves, not the way others see us.

Nevertheless, how God sees us and created us to be, like him, as sons and daughters in his image and likeness. Remember God is the creator and the maker; God created you and me in his own image and likeness.

Now you have an idea of how you should see you. Do not let the enemy and the evil one tell you who you are in Christ Jesus.

Prayer In The Spirit

Our heavenly father in the name of Jesus Christ I thank you for all that you have done and still doing for me, in me and through your Holy Spirit that works in me.

Lord I continue to pray in the spirit that you will strengthen me in my faith and love in you.

Lord Jesus continue to shine your light for my eyes to see, for my heart to hear and understand your will and love for me. Lord shine your light for my feet to follow you.

Lord let your Holy Spirit lead me, guide me and protect me from every other Spirit that is not from you.

Lord cover me with the blood from Jesus Christ, fill my heart with your wisdom of words, truth, strength, Holy Spirit, understanding, love and power to declare; and to do everything in your name.

Lord Jesus by your stripes I am healed and sickness cannot live in my body.

Lord, I pray that you will prepare the table before me in the presences of my enemies; Lord lead me not into temptation but deliver me from all evil. All the power, glory, honor, and praise are yours now and forever in the name of Jesus Christ, I pray.

Lord remove every desire of fear, darkness, lies, lust, pride and every other desire that is trying, and will try to stop me from doing what you have called me to do and be in your name. In Jesus name, I pray.

Lord fill my heart mind, spirit and soul with your desire, for me to give you all that I am and to resist the devil and the temptation in the world, this I ask in Jesus name.

Lord lead me to the cross where your love and blood was shed for me; and where the flood gates of heaven were opened washing away the powers of death.

Lord Jesus fill me with your light of salvation and grace to see and to know who is and not from you.

Lord my heart is yours, I am yours, I am not my own. Lord I pray that my faith and love in you will never fail and go cold, no matter what I may go through.

Lord I pray for the strength to seek you first and to stay awake in my Spirit and be ready when you come. Lord give me the tools, fill me with the strength and power to do your will.

Lord fill my mind with your thoughts, my heart and spirit with the power of your love and light to shine your Holy Spirit of truth, through me, in me and around me in the name of Jesus Christ.

Lord let the words of your Holy Spirit speak in me, so I can hear your voice in my spirit. Lead me by your Spirit Lord to stay focus and true.

Lord through thick and thin make me your instrument to be an overcomer like your son Jesus Christ. Lord Jesus, greater is he that is in me, than the one that is in the world.

I can do all things through Christ Jesus who gives me strength. Lord make in me a new heart, a steadfast spirit, a clean mind and a faithful spirit in the name of Jesus to praise and worship you always; in good and in bad days.

Lord, I receive your blessing, healing, love, peace, strength and your protection in my heart, spirit and soul in Jesus name.

Lord all the glory, all the praise, all worship and honor is yours now and forever in Jesus Christ name I pray, Amen.

Integrity Of Oneself

Integrity of a person is like a tree that bears its fruits. 1 John 3:18 (NIV) Dear children, let's not merely say that we love each other; let us show the truth by our action.

Hebrews 12:14 (KJV) Follow peace with all men, and holiness, without which no man shall see the Lord.

Moreover, holiness is the Lord and integrity is the Lord words; many of us will say whatever we like to others, but that does not mean what we say, we will do.

Likewise, a mouth opens and words come out with no action; example- a tree without roots would not stand, or bear any fruit that is good. Your action speaks so loud I can hear what you are saying.

A person may not remember what you have done or doing for them; but a person will not forget the way you make them feel. Therefore, watch your tongue and keep your mouth shut, and you will stay out of trouble. The tongue can bring death or life; those who love to talk will reap the consequences.

The words from the Lord are a lamp for my feet, a strong tower in my soul and spirit.

Set a good example for your children: Proverbs 20:7 (NIV) The Godly walk with integrity; blessed are their children who follow them.

Proverbs 20:6 (NIV) Many will say they are loyal friends, but who can find one who is truly reliable?

Likewise many will come and go but the Lord will never leave you or forsaken you.

Proverbs 2:6-8 (NIV) For the Lord grants wisdom! From his mouth come knowledge and understanding. He grants a treasure of common sense to the honest. He is a shield to those who walk with integrity. He guards the paths of the just and protects those who are faithful to him.

Poem Of Integrity

What is integrity? It is a word with action and with truth. Integrity from the clouds brings rain; integrity from the sun shines bright light; seek and you will find not words in vain, but light and truth in the one that never tells a lie, his name is Jesus Christ.

Dogs will return to its vomit, pigs will return to the mud and human beings will return to the dust until their final resting place. The integrity from my father shines in me with a feeling of energy, with a promise that flows in me with living water, and like an eagle floating into the sky. Integrity of a person is not the good they do; it is the good that come out from inside a person.

A Prayer To The Lord
For Deliverance

Our father who are in heaven thank you for all you are doing in me, around me, through me and for others. Thank you Lord Jesus for all you have done for me.

Lord Jesus have mercy on me, forgive me for all the things that I had done wrong, knowingly and unknowingly, to the temple you have given to me and to others.

Thank you for delivering me and setting me free through and in the name of your son Jesus Christ; Thank you Lord for the cross, you are my shield, my strength, my tower, my light and my all in your love forever.

Thank you for setting me free and for placing me on solid ground at the foot of the cross. Thank you Lord Jesus for washing me in your blood and for lifting me up above all problems.

Thank you Lord for the experience of suffering for you; Lord Jesus because of the love you have for me and the love I have for you. I also suffer because I believe in your name.

Thank you Lord Jesus for blessing me, and filling my Spirit with the confidence, the courage, the unchangeable promises of faith, endurance, love, spiritual growth and obedience in the name of Jesus Christ. I pray.

Lord, you are my joy and my strength; you make my heart glad and my spirit rejoices with your spirit of peace that lives in me forever.

Lord search me and download your will into my heart, my mind, my soul and my spirit to do what you have called me to do. Lord fill me with the history of your unfailing love, your wisdom and the understanding to know you more and to do more.

Lord shine your light and wash my heart with the blood from Jesus to stay loyal, to stay faithful, to Stay clean and to continue in worshiping you with the desire of an obedient, steadfast and loving Spirit in heart and in truth .

Lord let the words that comes from my mouth be the words from your Holy Spirit of love that speaks in my heart, in the name of Jesus.

Lord open my mind to understand your words in the scriptures (the Holy- Bible). Lord you are the stairway between heaven and earth.

Lord let the spirit that is in me, your Holy Spirit fill my heart with the power of fire to destroy every evil spirit and every weapon that form against me in the name of Jesus Christ.

In the name of Jesus Christ, I declare that every power of darkness will be cast out and bind into outer darkness of fire and never to be again.

Lord Jesus shine your light of protection around me, my family, my brothers, my sisters, my mother, my father, and every child and children of God in the name of Jesus.

Lord you are my first, my last, my refuge, my redeemer and the anchor for my soul. Lord fill my heart with your desire to seek you first and to stay faithful, putting all my faith and trust in you alone in the name of Jesus Christ, I pray and seal, Amen.

A Strong Heart

A heart that God has made within me, a heart that never stop loving; a heart that stays pure no matter what. A heart of light that shines love. A heart of love that never gets old. A happy heart, a joyful heart, a peaceful heart and a heart that has been made from the hands of love.

I was looking in and through the eyes of the soul. Seeing what God has stored there. Bow to no man or any kind, stand for what is yours, be strong and courageous. What you are thinking is not wrong, with a happy heart.

God made it all, with his creative and unfailing love; Feeling the presence of God everywhere. Never let your heart be trouble, by others. Sorrow awaits those who do evil.

The Lord holds me in his arms protecting me, and his strong army surrounds me. My heart said no weapon form against me, or come my way will ever prosper.

All I see is love, joy, happiness and peace in all I do and say from the heart to others. The strong heart of love. Thank you Lord Jesus.

The Motives Behind Being Generous

Proverbs 16:24 (NIV) Kind words are like a honey sweet to the soul and healthy for the body.

When people are stingy, they usually never realize it. You can give and still be stingy. Moreover, there are some people who give, but with a grudging heart. They think, do I have to give. There are some people who offer things, but in their mind, they hope the other person will say no.

We must not be lovers of self and lovers of money. We must think about others just like Christ thought about us. Give with a cheerful heart not expecting anything in return.

Be generous and love others just like Christ loves you. Stinginess is not part of the Christian life or any others life.

The world we are living in is becoming more selfish and people are showing their true colors. Furthermore, how they give and what they give.

Example- there is a saying, I give you something and do something for you; you have to do something for me in return.

We always think about ourselves even when doing something for others. I am not saying do not think about yourself, I am just saying do not be all about self.

2 Corinthians 9:7-10 (NIV) You must each decide in your heart how much to give. And don't give reluctantly or in response to pressure. "For God loves a person who gives cheerfully." And God will generously provide all you need. Then you will always have everything you need and plenty left over to share with others.

As the scriptures say, "they share freely and give generously to the poor. Their good deeds will be remembered forever." For God is the one who provides seeds for the farmer and then bread to eat. In the same way, he will provide and increase your resources and then produce a great harvest of generosity in you.

Proverbs 22:9 (NIV) The generous will themselves be blessed, for they share their food with the poor.

Luke 6:38(NIV) Give, and you will receive. Your gift will return to you in full pressed down, shaken together to make room for more, running over, and poured into your lap. The amount you give will determine the amount you get back.

Proverbs 21:13 (NIV) Those who shut their ears to the cries of the poor will be ignored in their own time of need.

Proverbs 19:17 (NIV) If you help the poor, you are lending to the Lord and he will pay you!

Brotherly love. Proverbs 17:17 (KJV) A friend loveth at all times, and a brother is born for adversity. Many of us give and speak, to look good in the eyes of other people.

Furthermore, many of us like to be noticed, and like to seek praise for what we do and say. The Bible say do not let the right hand see what the left hand is doing.

To illustrate a little more; when many people are seen doing good things, that does not mean that they are good; good things do not come from the outside, it comes from the inside and show on the outside.

Example: a good tree does not bear bad fruit and a bad tree cannot bear good fruit. Many who are pretending to do good and be good; the only praise they will get is from man.

God knows the heart; (Proverbs 16:2 (NIV) People may be pure in their own eyes, but the Lord examines their motives.

Proverbs 21:2 (NIV) People may be right in his own eyes, but the Lord examines the heart.

Proverbs 30:12 (NIV) They are pure in their own eyes, but they are filthy and unwashed.

Proverbs 11:1 (KJV) A false balance is an abomination to the Lord, but a just weight is his delight.

Loving Me To Love Others

Romans 13:8-10 (NIV) Owe nothing to anyone, except for your obligation to love one another. If you love your neighbor, you will fulfill the requirements of God's law.

For the commandments say, you must not commit adultery. You must not murder. You must not steal. You must not covet. These and other commandment, are summed up in this one commandment; Love your neighbor as yourself. Love does no wrong to others, so love is the fulfills the requirements of God's law.

Loving me is so beautiful; I love me, because God first love me. The most important feeling is, I love the Lord, and I know God loves me. I love my life now, for I was dead but now I was brought back to life. I am a child of God. I love nature because I am part of nature. I can say I am grateful, for the life I have, and continuing to live.

Thank you Lord. I am a free spirit full of love and the joy of the Lord. I am blessed to live my own life, and to make my own choice and choices. Loving me is one of the most important and beautiful feeling I ever felt and know. I greet myself every day and every night. I am beautiful from the inside out.

I love me just like the wind, when it blows. I love me... I am one with the source of love and life. The source of love is within me, and around me.

I love me for all that is there to love. I cannot waste my time on negative thoughts, and negative energy.

When I picture my life from then to now, I can say I have always seen the beauty of God love for my life shining in me. Most people will come up to me and ask. Who are you; my reply to them is.... I am a child of the living God of Jesus Christ.

I am one full of love to share with you and others. I am a child that came from the source of love, joy, happiness, and peace.

My heart is full of love. Every time my heart beats, I will take a minute to listen to the sweet music that plays. Feeling the energy of love floating into the air, so pure kind and peaceful.

Love is all I have to give. Love came from the Lord. Loving me is like a river that never stop flow; from a bottomless sea, from a heart of divine love. No end to his love, it only goes around and around, until it reaches its next chapter to love again.

Loving me should not be a hard thing to do. The way I love me is the way I will love you. Loving me is part of being me. My life is full of God blessing and love. If I do not love me who will love me? Love... what is love. Love is God, and God is love, that is true love. Love is one self in the one who loves me.

Loving me, makes me look conceded in the eyes of others. It is ok, only haters hate. If loving me is wrong, then what is right, loving me? Loving me, is loving the one who created me. The reflection of love reflects in others and in me. I am happy with who I am.

My experience of loving me comes from God. The image of me is the image of God. I will never stop loving me. Loving me is an open door for the

Lord to enter. *Many are trying to stop me, from loving me. It will never happen, or take root. No one will know or understand, what loving me means, until they know how to love their own self within.*

Loving me is a free will of God. The only person who will tell me, loving me is wrong is Satan, the devil, who does not know a thing about love. Furthermore, who can say they love someone, truly love someone? However, and they do not love themselves.

I love me, because I found me in love, and love in me; Love was sowed and planted into me like a seed; and love is still growing within me. Love took birth in me, before I was even born. The compassion of love was given to me, now and forever to share.

Loving me is not a coincident; it is a gift from God through Jesus Christ. It was a price bought and paid for with love for you and me. Loving me is the root in my heart, soul and spirit. I was conceived with love and I will die with love. Love will never depart, are be taken away from me.

Loving me, have a strong hold on me. Loving me brings the presence, of the source of love to others. When I die, love will live on. Loving me is eternal. Love is not a word or a feeling it is an action. Loving me brings everything around me with love. Loving me brings light into my life and light into the world.

I am blessed to find your love in me Lord. There is no question about loving me. Loving me is a grateful feeling you created inside me. As long as I live, I will be sharing the free will of God love. Loving me was not taken; it was given to me, all I had to do was allow it to be.

Looking, into my own eyes, and seeing my soul, it showed me how to see how beautiful and loving I am. Loving me change everything around me.

Loving me is pure in the things I feel. Loving me is the resurrection of love and life. Loving me is my job.

Loving me is part of taking care of the temple of the Lord. Loving me, make me see life, and the things around me clearly.

Loving me, helped me to find the key for true... love, joy, happiness, peace, and freedom in the Lord. Loving me is the resurrection of being dead to life through Christ our Lord. I have to do what I feel in my heart. The heart does not lie; true love is in the eyes of the most high God of our Lord Jesus Christ.

I am going to move forward by having a relationship with the Lord Jesus, and being grateful for all the things, he have given and shared with me; likewise, the love Jesus showed and teaches me how to love not only me but also one another.

Loving me is part of doing what I love. Loving me is a connection with the Lord. Loving me is a covenant with the Lord forever. Loving me is feeling the love of the Lord moving into my heart; furthermore feeling the tears of love falling and over flowing into love.

Loving me is my green light to go. Loving me is accepting me, for who I am and who God says I am. Moreover, not what others and the world may think and say about me.

Loving me brings answer to my entire question. Loving me is a new journey of my life. Loving me is awakening in love through love. The truth about loving me is loving he who first loves me; and loving one another as I love my self.

Jesus Christ is the light that shines the love of life through you and me so we can live in love with one another. Loving me is loving God, in the name of our Lord Jesus Christ to love you.

The Unknown

The unknown is the fear of the darkness in our heart. The illusion of the hole we have dug. The illusion from the belief of others.

The unknown is what we do not see but believe. The spirit of the unknown that lives within thy self is stronger than the unknown that lives in this world.

The best thing about the unknown is we get to hope for something better. In addition for the best not only for ourselves but for others too.

We get to experience something new; a challenge and something beautiful.

The unknown is the light, we are searching for; the unknown is believing what the eyes cannot see. The unknown is one we search for with faith. The unknown is what you do not know.

However, what you about to find out. The unknown is Jesus Christ our Lord; if you do not know him, now is the best time to get to know him. He is the king of all kings and the Lord of all Lord.

Prayer To Be Filled With
The Holy Spirit

Dear Lord Jesus, I thank you for giving your life on the cross and for your blood that was shed for me. I place my whole being into your hands. I humbly ask you to fill me with your Holy Spirit, to stay with me always, to help and to guide me.

Lord, help me to be open, to listen and follow where your spirit guides me. I ask this in Jesus name, Amen.

Who I Am

That is a very good question. I am what I am. I am a question mark. I am a flower in the garden. I am a free Spirit of divine love. When I came into the world, I been taught so many things, and learn some many things about who I am. To my understanding, I am a child from the most high God, the creator of all life through our Lord Jesus Christ.

I am an authentic being that cannot be copied and be labeled; I am a spiritual being created in the image and likeness of God the father.

Essence vs personality what is the essence of who you are? Example-essence is an effort of existing; a living thing that has (or can develop) the ability to act or function independently.

Personality is an effort to deceive, the complex of all the attributes-- temperamental, emotional and mental—that characterize a unique individual.

When you stay true and authentic, you would not have to worry and wonder who you are, and what others may tell you who, and what you are to be.

Furthermore, you and I are not a counterfeit and we cannot be copied; moreover, you and I are a natural signature from God. We are God masterpiece. We were made and created by the word of our heavenly father of our Lord Jesus.

The desire of life is to be, not to become; as I said authentic and not a counterfeit. We all as human beings have some kind of personality. There are many kinds of personality in a person. One- Personality of being authentic and natural.

Two- personality of being a counterfeit and unnatural. A counterfeit personality will deceive you and others. Example- not everything that glitters is gold.

To illustrate a little more on the topic, the personality from the devil is to kill, steal and destroy; his personality is to deceive.

Why, is that because he is the father of all lies, the deceiver? The prince of the air. He comes in the form of a light on the outside, but within he is full of darkness. Moreover, he is a wolf in sheep clothing.

The personality of God, the father of our Lord Jesus Christ, is life, love, peace and light. He is the light to shine his love for all to see and be true in Spirit. Jesus is the light of the world. All who believes in him is a reflection of him.

Who am I, I am a doctor, a lawyer, a police officer, a writer, and so on. Life is so beautiful in the eyes of many of us, especially when we can become any and everything we desire.

The desire of life in the world, is to be everything but ourselves; that is what been taught to us from an early age, who and what we should be. Moreover, many of us do not know the differences in who we are, and what we do, are not the same. As I said earlier, I am a doctor, a Lawyer, a police officer, a writer and so on.

However, when I thought about all that I had just said that I am. I am an image of God through our Lord Jesus, and the things I said that I am earlier; it relates to a profession of work and service that many of us participate in and do.

One In One

One in one is love. One in one is peace. One in one is togetherness. One in one is whole. One in one is joy. One in one is God. Look deep within love and you will see love.

One in one is happiness. One in one is grace. One in one is respect. One in one is freedom. One in one is where the spirit lives.

Love been told to everyone. Love was given to everyone. When we were babies, we were love, we got love, even before we were even born, we been love. Now is time to find love, from the one that is within one.

One in one is a word. One in one is an action. One in one is to say I am love. One in one is to show love. Furthermore, when you find one in one, Life will change into love.

One in one is a smile that will take you to that mile. One in one is life, sowing a seed of one in one, has to die before it can give life again.

When you seek, you will find the one in one in you. The first and the last, the three in one have now became the one in one, in you and in me; moreover, not to fall in love but to rise in love.

A Prayer To Be Restored

Father God in the name of Jesus Christ, I will like to thank you for hearing my prayer and for giving me access to come to you as I am. I pray and ask you to restore me in every area of my life and everything that the enemy has stolen and taken away from me. In Jesus name, I pray.

Lord Jesus I pray that when my enemies come one way to attack me, they will flee seven ways; I pray that when my enemies come before me Lord you will put me behind them and when they come behind me you will put me before them.

Lord Jesus I pray that you will make all my crooked ways straight. Lord you are all I want, need and have. Lord Jesus, you hold me in the palm of your hands with love and with a never-ending protection of light, peace, love and joy with your promises.

Lord Jesus I believe in you, Lord I belong to you; Lord the joy of your name have given me the strength; Lord your words flows in me with songs of peace, love and with the river of living water.

Lord, you are the reason I live; Lord you live in me with a light of victory, a light that will never goes out.

Lord nothing cannot separate me from you and the love you have for me. Lord Jesus baptized me with the water, your blood, the power and fire of your Holy Spirit, restore me Lord. This I pray and ask in the name of Jesus Christ. Amen.

The Judge

Who is the judge? We are all a judges. Why did you ask that question? (Simple) – I think every human being is a judge of him and herself.

In the beginning, the word of God gave life; and up to this present day, he is still giving life, and he is renewing lives as we speak. Likewise, life is God and God is life, by his word, he made you and me.

When life was given birth to all things by the word of God; including you, everything and me. It was given to us with a choice of free will. A choice to make, take and be responsible for the things we do and say. Moreover, the life we choose to live and the relationship we have with God.

A fool will say in his and her heart, that there is no God. Example) many of us will ask the question- why there is light and why the trees are green. Many of us will have an readymade answer why there is light and why the trees are green.

Many of us as human being think we have all the answers and know it all, even when we do not know; we will make up an answer for the questions. Moreover, we start to pass judgement why the trees are green; the trees are green because of this and because of that.

In life somethings are what they are, furthermore, somethings are the way they are. Moreover, many of us cannot and will not accept that it is what it is, and it is the way it is.

Indeed, we all as human beings love to judge and pass judgement on others and on things. There is an old saying do not sale, what does not belong to you. We can judge everything and find out the detail and information about everything and everyone.

Nevertheless, it is hard for us to see ourselves the way we see everything we pass judgement on. It is easy to notice the notice; but when the notice, notice us, it become a mirror of the notice looking back.

Matthew 7:1-5 (NIV) Do not judge others, and you will not be judged. For you will be treated as you treat others. The standard you use in judging is the standard by which you will be judged.

And why worry about a speck in your friends eye when you have a log in your own? How can you think of saying to your friend? Let me help you get rid of that speck in your eye; when you cannot see past the fog in your own eyes.

Hypocrite! Frist get of the log in your own eyes; then you will see well enough to deal with the speck in your friend eyes.

God is love and those who live in God, God lives in them. The awareness of life is a light through our Lord Jesus Christ, who has been sent by our heavenly Father to share his love and to open our heart to do the same with one another.

Jesus is the only way; he is the way the truth and the life, the bread of life, the tree of life. Moreover, by the tree you will know its fruit.

God will always win his victory over evil, evil is the root of our faith; the words of Jesus Christ come true before our eyes every day and will continue to come true until the end of time.

Blessed is he who obeys his commandments to love one another and make a better world by the grace of our Lord Jesus Christ be with us all.

We are all hypocrite in some way, many of us seem to be shinning like a light; but inward we are full of darkness.

Likewise, wolf in sheep clothing, judging not ourselves, but others. when we are doing the same things. If we look deep within ourselves, we will get to see the reflection of our self in the mirror calling us out of the darkness into the light.

In the beginning, God created the heavens, the earth and everything in them. God created man from the ground; he breathed the breath of life into man nostrils and man became a living person.

The Lord God placed the man in the Garden of Eden to tend and watch over it. However, the Lord warned him, you may freely eat the fruit of every tree in the garden except the tree of the knowledge of good and evil. If you eat its fruit, you are sure to die. Than the Lord God said, it is not good for man to be alone. I will make him a helper who is just right for him.

The story continues in Genesis 3; moreover, man was put to the test, in the Garden of Eden. Where the man and woman had, the choice and free will in making the right judgement, in the responsibility the creator has given them in obeying his command.

To make a long story short. There was a serpent in the Garden of Eden; the serpent was the shrewdest of all the animals the Lord God had made. One day the serpent asked the woman, did God really say you must not eat the fruit from any of the trees in the garden, the woman replied. It is only the fruit from the tree in the middle of the Garden that we are not allowed to eat.

The serpent continues to talk to the woman telling her she will not die if she touch the tree and eat the fruit, that God told them not to eat from.

The serpent also told the woman you would not die but your eyes will be open as soon as you eat it. He said God know your eyes will open and you will be like God, knowing good and evil.

After all had said and done the woman was convince, she saw the fruit looked good, so she took the fruit and eat it and give to the man who was with her and he also eat.

Moreover, their eyes were open, they felt shame at their nakedness so they sewed fig leaves together to cover themselves and hide themselves. When the cool evening breeze was bowing, the man and his wife heard the Lord God among the trees.

Than they heard, the voice of God called to the man, where are you? He replied, I heard you walking in the garden so I hid. I was afraid because I was naked.

Who told you that you were naked? The Lord asked. Have you eaten from the tree whose fruit I commanded you not to eat. The man replied, it was the woman you gave me who gave me the fruit, and I ate it.

Than the Lord God asked the woman, what have you done? The serpent deceive me," she replied. That is why I ate it. Than the Lord God said to the serpent, because you have done this, you are curse more than all the animals, domestic and wild.

The Lord God had pass judgement on the serpent for what he had done in deceiving the woman. The Lord said to the serpent you are cursed.

When the Lord God had asked the man if he have eaten from the tree, he has commanded him not to eat from. The man replied the woman you gave me who gave me the fruit and I ate it. Than the Lord God asked the woman what have you done.

In the same way The Lord God will asked every one of us what have we done. To illustrate a little more, whom will you blame; there will not be anyone to blame and judge but thy self.

In all that has been said and done; the God of our Lord Jesus Christ is the judge of everything seen and unseen. There will be a time and a place when we all as human being, would have to answer to the creator for all the things we have said, and done on earth; moreover, to the body God has breath the breathe of life into you and me.

Prayer To The Lord

Father God in the name of your son Jesus Christ, I pray in thanking you for your love, the breath of life, your grace, your forgiveness and for opening your arms of love for me to come to you in Spirit and in truth.

Lord Jesus I open the door to my heart for you to come in, come Lord Jesus come in me.

Lord Jesus I pray that you will send your legions of warrior angels to protect and surround me with your fire of light, love and your clouds to clothed me with the shadow of your wings of peace and joy.

Lord I have seen and tasted your love and the presences of joy into your atmosphere with peace.

Lord your glory, your love and protection are what my heart needs to overcome the things that are not from you. Lord Jesus fill me with the sword of your Spirit and your words as a shield of protection and a lamp for my feet. Lord let your will be done in me.

Father God there is nothing worth more, and worthy than you and the love you have for others and me. In the name of Jesus Christ, I pray and declare that there is nothing that could compare to what you can do. Lord, you are everything to me and you are everywhere I am, you are my shelter Lord.

Lord Jesus what is impossible with man is possible with you. Lord Jesus I cannot run away from you, but to you. You are all I have, you are the way the truth and the life. You are my father, my refuge, my rock, my fortress, my pride, my joy and my strength.

Father God in the name of our Lord Jesus Christ I ask you to renew the inner man (Spirit) within me to see and to be aware of the things, which are seen eternal in the plans you have for my life.

Lord Jesus guide me into your way, put into my heart your desires and will for my life; strengthen me by your Holy Spirit to walk by faith not by sight.

Lord plant and write your words into my heart, so I can worship you In spirit and in truth. Lord give me day by day, comfort for my soul, peace for my mind, Spirit and light for my feet. Lord let my heart rejoice and overflow with the joy of your salvation.

Lord Jesus protect me from my enemies, lead me away from temptation and guide me into your light.

All the power, honor, worship, glory and praise are your forever and ever in the name of Jesus I pray. You are God alone; before the world begins, you were on your throne.

Lord Jesus draw me close to you, to the cross, clothed me with your Spiritual clothing of love, protection, light, forgiveness and with the blood of Jesus Christ;

Lord cover my head with the of helmet of salvation, the armor of protection, fill me with the sword of the Spirit, the joy of your salvation, the breastplate of righteousness, the faith and peace; the power of your words in the blood and cross of life, in the name of Jesus Christ I declare and bind over me.

Lord cover me with the shadow of your wings, and anchor your words into my heart from the stormy sea.

Lord let your glory shines, like lighten from one end of the earth to the other side, for all to see the victory in the cross were your love and blood were shed for us. Lord Jesus I pray for freedom and I declare it in the name of Jesus Christ.

Thank you Lord Jesus for setting me free from the bondage of me and the bondage from the things in the unseen world. This I pray and seal over and in my life with your blood Lord, in the name of Jesus Christ, Amen.

Elected By Men Or Appointed By God

Father God in the name of our Lord Jesus, I thank you for your love, your Grace, your wisdom and your understanding to know the truth in your words and in your son Jesus Christ.

I thank you father God for your wisdom and your understanding to see and to know the tree by the fruit it bear, and to see who is and not from you.

Lord Jesus continue to guide me into your path way of life and fill me with the power of your Holy Spirit for my life.

I want to examine some personal nature of false ministers so that we can recognize them and avoid them. Furthermore, seeing the tree by the fruit it bears.

Moreover, many people have been elected by men to do the work of God, by using human understanding and saying God has sent them. Likewise preaching man-made wisdom, but not the kingdom of God.

What is the root cause of division within the Christion faith and churches? I see all traditional church leaders are using enticing words of man-made wisdom. Furthermore, preaching and teaching the doctrine and the commandments of men.

Jeremiah 17:9-10 (NIV) The human heart is the most deceitful of all things, and desperately wicked. Who really knows how bad it is.

But I, the Lord, search all hearts and examine secret motives. I give all people their due rewards according to what their action deserve.

Matthew 15:8-9 (NIV) These people honor me with their lips, but their hearts are far from me.

Matthew 15:13 (NIV) Jesus replied, every plant not planted by my heavenly father will be uprooted.

Acts 5:29 (NIV) But peter and the apostles replied, we must obey God rather than any human authority.

1 Corinthians 1: 10 (NIV) I appeal to you, dear brothers and sisters, by the authority of our Lord Jesus Christ, to live in harmony with each other. Let there be no divisions in the church. Rather, be of one mind, united in thought and purpose.

James 4:7-8 (NIV) So humble (submit) yourselves before God. Resist the devil, and he will flee from you. Come close to God, and God will come close to you. Wash your hands, you sinners; purify your hearts, for your loyalty is divided between God and the world.

2 Timothy 4:3-4 (NIV) For the time is coming when people will not endure sound teaching, but having itching ears they will accumulate for themselves teachers to suit their own passions, and will turn away from listening to the truth and wander off into myths.

Romans 12:2 (NIV) Don't copy the behavior and customs of this world, but let God transform you into a new person by changing the way you think. Then you will learn to know God's will for you, which is good and pleasing and perfect.

Jesus said many false prophets and Christ would come in his name. Jesus also said do not let anyone mislead you, for many will come in his name, claiming, I am the messiah.

1 John 4:1-6 (NIV) Dear friend, do not believe everyone who claims to speak by the Spirit. You must test them to see if the Spirit they have comes from God: for there are many false prophets in the world.

This is how we know if they have the Spirit of God: if a person claiming to be a prophet acknowledges that Jesus Christ came in a real body, that person has the Spirit of God.

But if someone claims to be a prophet and does not acknowledges the truth about Jesus, that person is not from God. Such person has the Spirit of the antichrist, which you heard is coming into the world and indeed is already here.

But you belong to God, my dear children. You have already won the victory over those people, because the spirit who lives in you is greater than the spirit who lives in the world, so they speak from the world's viewpoint, and the world listens to them.

But we belong to God, and those who know God listen to us. If they do not belong to God, they do not listen to us, that is how we know if someone has the Spirit of truth or the Spirit of deception.

1 Thessalonians 5:20-22 (NIV) Do not scoff at prophecies, but test everything that is said. Hold on to what is good. Stay away from every kind of evil.

Now the spirit speak expressly, that in the latter times some shall depart from the faith, giving heed to seducing spirits, and doctrines of devils;

In the world we are living in today, the things we are experiencing and seeing is nothing new. Moreover, everything that is happening now has been happening long before we even exited.

Likewise, generation after generation, changing like the weather and the season. I pray in the name of our Lord Jesus Christ, that you will seek first the kingdom of God about all, and live righteously, and he will give you everything you need.

Prayer For Thanksgiving

Lord Jesus, you are worthy to be praise, you are all I wanted, and you are what my heart desire. All the glory, the honor and the power is yours.

Lord Jesus as I walk through the valley of the shadow of death I shall fear no evil, for I know you are here with me, your rod and staff they comfort me; in the presences of my enemies. I will call upon your name, in thanksgiving and in praising you; Lord with joy and for your protection with the covering of the blood of Jesus Christ.

Lord Jesus as I enter into your gates with thanksgiving and go into your courts with praise. Lord Jesus your unfailing love continues forever and ever with your faithfulness to each generation.

Thank you Lord Jesus. All the glory, power and honor is your Lord; my soul sing and worship you with the joy you made it with and the love you created into my heart.

My soul and spirit rejoice with every beat of my heart, where your love overflows Lord. Thank you Lord Jesus, may your spirit be with us all in love, unity, peace, joy and one family. In the name of Jesus I pray, Amen.

My Heart

My heart beat so hard and so loud. All I have to give is love. Love is everything to me; how hard is it to love everyone and everything God have created; God is love he created you and me with love, in love. Therefore, you are and I am love.

God of our Lord Jesus Christ loves everyone and everything he created. God created everyone and everything with his love. The Love of God has taken over me with a feeling I cannot express with word but with action.

When you have love to give you cannot and will not hold it back. Love is the way to everything. Jesus is the way the truth and the life.

All I can do is breath love. Feel love and give love; my heart feels like exploring. The heart cries love and then over flowing with joy. The power of love lives inside of me like lightening.

The vibration of the thunder has shaken and awakens me up from the darkness to the light; many are called with the feeling of love floating in the air, as the clouds shares the blessing of the love God have given you and me.

My heart never sleeps it only beat and pump love, joy, happiness, peace and much more.

The love of God runs through my heart and my veins like a river. It never stops flowing, but it only over flows; sowing and reaping kindness of love. The energy of love is so beautiful to me; it has taken me everywhere; where the love of Jesus meets.

Moreover, having no fear and knowing in my heart; who I am and why I am here? I am only here to share the gift of love to all. My heart smiles a mile, whenever I give and share the love of God to everyone; Love cannot be taken away From a happy heart.

My heart were made by the hands of God the almighty father with love; Filling an empty room with the presence of peace and love; Nowhere to run, but to surrender all, Compassion of love lives on, knocking on every heart.

I cannot hold back what the heart feels, God touch me in a special way. He has given me a gift to love; why should I be Selfish with what I have to give or say.

Who feels it, knows it. I keep my eyes on the light of love as the angles carry me safety showing me who I am in God.

I am a child and an image of his likeness, nothing but love in everything he has made me to be and to do, in his name; God is love.

Greater is he who lives in me is greater than he who lives in the world. Being near and far, in and out; my heart is open to love, cannot be shut knowing who I am in love and in Christ Jesus. Knowing where love has taken me and where it came from. In a place where happy hearts meets and join in love.

Prayer to the Lord

Lord Jesus thank you for all you have done and still doing for others and me. Lord Jesus you are the Holy and eternal one who was and is to come. Lord Jesus, the first and the last, the righteous and holy one, the prince of peace, the name above all names.

My spirit is here to worship you Lord Jesus. Lord, the wonders of your mighty love have brought me peace and comfort for my soul.

Lord nothing can compare to the love you have for me. My hope is built on nothing else than you Lord. The promise in your name is a shield and a protection for my soul. Lord Jesus there is nothing in the world that can compare to the love you have for me;

Lord Jesus there is nothing that can satisfy me but only you. The promise in your name is a shield, an anchor and a protection for my spirit and soul. Lord my heart sings and rejoices at the work of your hands. The beauty of your name is a sweet taste of freedom.

I am forgiving by confessing, by repenting and believing in the name of Jesus Christ. I am justify by faith. Yes Lord Jesus I am healed by your stripes; I am covered and wash with your blood Lord Jesus.

Lord Jesus I am healed with the healing power of your Holy Spirit that lives within me. I am saved by your grace through salvation and repentance; on the cross at which you die Lord Jesus. I am free and cleanse with your blood.

Father God in the name of your son Jesus, I thank you for revealing yourself to me in the spirit of love. Lord, I was searching all eternity and I could not find anyone like you; the love, the peace, the joy and the freedom I found in you.

Lord my heart and spirit will praise you every day and always. Lord the angels and the saints sing and praise you, today, tomorrow and every other day until the end of time in the mighty name of Jesus.

Lord, you have given it all for me on the cross. My heart cries out with the desire to be with you where you are. I just want to say thank you Lord, for the way you loves me.

Our faithful and merciful father of our Lord Jesus Christ; whom you have sent to pay the price for our sins on the cross. Thank you Lord for your grace and your unfailing love. Thank you Lord.

Lord, you knew me before I was formed in my mother womb. Lord Jesus you have risen me up in the beauty of your name. Lord my soul found refuge, strength, love, forgiveness, unity and peace in the power of the mighty cross, in the name of Jesus Christ I pray. Amen.

A Star

Catching a falling star, from the ego of the mind. Saying there is no exit, when you enter. Leasing a plan to make more. Buying a permit for freedom. Selling a soul for an empty world. Drowning, in our own shame, pointing fingers, no one to blame.

A mirror calls you out. Shipping and receiving as a product. A frame of memories is where you hang. A memory is what remains, or what will be. Stand your ground and then you will see.

Before you sign, make sure you read it properly. Count your blessing with love, and it will set you free.

Jesus lives in you and Jesus lives in me. Put your trust and faith in God and you will never be the same. Do not gain the world and lose your soul.

Prayer-My Soul Thirsts
For You O God

Psalms 63:1-8 (KJV) O God, thou art my God; early I seek thee; my soul thirsteth for thee; my flesh longeth for thee in a dry and thirsty land, where no water is. To see thy power and thy glory, I have seen thee in the sanctuary. Because thy lovingkindness power better than life, my lips will praise thee.

Thus will I bless thee while I live; I will lift up my hands in thy name. My soul shall be satisfied as with marrow and fatness; and my mouth shall praise thee with joyful lips;

When I remember thee upon my bed, and meditate on thee in the night watches. Because thou hast been my help, therefore in the shadow of thy wings will I rejoice. My soul followeth hard after thee; thy right hand upholdeth me.

Are You Safe?

Heavenly father of our Lord Jesus Christ, thank you for the breath of life. 1 Corinthians 6:17 (NIV) But the person who is joined to the Lord becomes one spirit with him.

In the heart of every person, there is a desire to be safe and secure. Little children are often afraid of being left alone. They also may fear the dark, or the unknown. The younger children as well as the older ones crave the security of being held in the loving embrace of their parents.

There they feel confident and protected. As we mature, the desire to be safe and secure never leaves us. The inborn desire was given to us by our creator. While some men and women act fearless, in their hearts they may fear the unknown, suffering, accident, or sickness. The list can go on.

They may also have an uneasy feeling about what might happen to them after death. God is the creator of heaven and earth; making man was the crowning act of his creation.

God place Adam and his wife Eve in a paradise home called the Garden of Eden. They were secure, happy, peaceful and free. Then Satan, who appeared in the form of a serpent, deceived them and they sinned. Because of their disobedience to God, they fell out of fellowship with him and were driven from Eden.

What a drastic change! Before, they had been safe and without fear. Adam and Eve they were at peace with their creator, enjoying his presence.

Now, instead of inner peace, there was unrest, guilt, and fear. They were afraid of God and hid from him! They had experienced spiritual death, which is separation from God.

When fellowship with God was broken through disobedience, there was deep distress in the hearts of Adam and Eve. Only fellowship with the living God can satisfy the soul.

Moreover, man's inner conflict has also caused all manner of outward conflict, often resulting in murder or war. There has always been much strife on earth; one tribe quarrels with another, one nation strives to bring another nation under its rule.

In these conflicts, one nation has always emerged victorious, only weaken later and become subject to another nation. The prophet Daniel says, that the living may know that the most high rule in the kingdom of men, and giveth it to whomever he will. In addition, remove kings, and set up kings.

The safety of our nation depends less upon its military might and more upon prevalence of righteousness and the fear of God among its people.

Proverbs 19:23 (NIV) Fear of the Lord leads to life, bringing security and protection from harm.

Our personal safety is a separate matter. We can have an inner security that no earthly nation can offer.

John 18:36 (KJV) Jesus answered, my kingdom is not of this world: if my kingdom were of this world, then would my servants fight, that I should not be delivered to the Jews: but now is my kingdom not from hence.

The kingdoms of this world are in the God's hands and will not endure forever. Our personal relationship with God is of a different dimension.

When we are in God's kingdom, we are in a kingdom that is not subject to success or failure of any earthly nation. His kingdom is much more secure than any superpower.

There we are safe, regardless of what happens to any nation. Kingdom will rise and fall.

John 10:29 (KJV) My father, which gave them me, is greater than all; and no man is able to pluck them out of my father's hand.

According to bible prophecy, 2 Timothy 3:13 (KJV) But evil men and seducers shall wax worse and worse, deceiving, and being deceived.

The future offers no security. The strife and turmoil around the world may grow worse as eternity approaches. There is a day coming in which God has determined that there should be a time no longer.

In 2 peter 3: 10 (KJV) But the day of the Lord will come as a thief in the night; in which the heavens shall pass away with a great noise, and the elements shall melt with fervent heat, the earth also and the works that are therein shall be burned up.

The Holy Scriptures say that every knee shall bow, and that all men will be gathered before the throne of the almighty Jude.

On that great judgement; Matthew 24:35 (KJV) Heaven and earth shall pass away, but my words shall not pass away.

No earthly power will be able to give us safety. All people shall bow before the great king and be judged. No caves or fortresses will be able to protect those who seek refuge in them.

All means of transportation will be useless. There will be no reassuring wail of sirens; no emergency or law enforcement personnel rushing to our rescue.

You and I will face the great judge all alone. At that point, our only safety will be if our name is written in the book of life in heaven. Our names are written in this book when we repent of our sins and believe in Jesus Christ.

God then forgives us and we are cleansed through his precious blood, which was shed on the cross that the whole world could be saved. We are then accepted as children of God.

God's children are not exempt from sickness or suffering. They may even lose their lives, but they need not fear because they are safe in the arms of Jesus.

Romans 8:28 (KJV) And we know that all things work together for good to them that love God, to them who are called according to his purpose.

Do you long for security do you have deep inner yearnings that you cannot satisfy. Although the soul longs for God, the sinful nature of man and women reaches for fleshly desires.

Isaiah 57:20-21 (KJV) But those who still reject me are the restless sea, which is never still but continually churns up mud and dirt. There is no peace for the wicked says God.

In this conflict, too many people follow the path of least resistance and make a decision by indecision. Finally, they slip from life into death and face a long eternity.

Real and lasting peace can only be found when we surrender mind, body and spirit to the one who has made us and loves us.

God is not only the master of the world, but he knows our lives from the beginning to the end. Jesus came into this world; Luke 1:79 (KJV) To give light to them that sit in darkness and in the shadow of death, to guide our feet into the way of peace.

Jesus suffered and shed his precious blood so that we can have peace and security.

Psalms 91:9-12 (NIV) If you make the Lord your refuge, if you make the most high your shelter, no evil will conquer you; no plague will come near your home. For he will order his angels to protect you wherever you go. they will hold you up with their hands so you won't even hurt your foot on a stone.

Do you feel the weight of sin in your heart? Do you worry about the future? On the other hand, do you try to block it out of your mind? Are you burdened with more than you can bear? Do you desire to be safe and secure?

Jesus said (Matthew 7:7 (KJV) Ask, and it shall be given to you; seek, and you shall find; knock, and it shall be opened unto you.

John 16:33 (NIV) I have told you this so that you may have peace in me. Here on earth you will have many trials and sorrows. But take heart, because I have overcome the world.

The Lord has a remedy for our sins. Jesus is the great burden- bearer, and nothing is too difficult for him.

Acts 3:19 (NIV) Now repent of your sins and turn to God, so that your sins may be wiped away.

Moreover when the times of refreshing shall come from the presence of the Lord. God speaking through the prophet Jeremiah, promised.

Jeremiah 29:11-13 (NIV) For I know the plans I have for you, says the Lord. They are plans for good and not for disaster, to give you a future and a hope. In those days when you pray, I will listen. If you look for me wholeheartedly, you will find me.

Prayer To The Lord

Father God in the name of your son Jesus Christ; I just want to say thank you for everything. Lord Jesus I take your precious blood and sprinkle it over myself and my family right from the crown of our heads to the soles of our feet, in Jesus name.

Lord Jesus I claim total and complete protection for my life and my family. Lord Jesus keep me free today from evil, sin, temptation, Satan's attacks and affliction, fear of darkness, fear of man, sickness, diseases, doubts, anger, all calamities and from all that is not of thy kingdom.

In the name of Jesus, I pray father God to fill me with your gift of the Holy Spirit and grant me the gift of wisdom, knowledge, understanding and discernment so that I will live today in your glory by doing what is right. In the name of Jesus Christ, I declare, believe and receive. Amen.

A Savior Or The Savior

2 Peter 3:9 (NIV) The Lord isn't really being slow about his promise, as some people think. No he is being patient, for your sake. He does not want anyone to be destroyed, but wants everyone to repent.

We are living in a world where many are looking for a savior or some kind; however, everyone can be a savior but it will only be for a while.

There is only one savior and his name is Jesus Christ; I hope you understand what I am saying here. Jesus is the savior for everything including you and me. I am speaking about the, not, a.

The two difference between the word (the savior) and the letter a savior. The word savior is permanent full time) and the letter a is temporary for a time.

Acts 4:12 (NIV) There is salvation in no one else! God has given no other name under heaven by which we must be saved among men by which we must be saved.

Are you a happy person? On the other hand, does guilt and fear overcome all your happiness? You wish you could get rid of your guilt, but how. Many of us go into this wondering mode, am I ever going to be happy again.

I have good news for you! There is someone who can help you, forgive your sins, and give you ever-lasting happiness. His name is Jesus. Let me tell you and enlighten you about him.

God is the one who made the world. He made everything in the world. He made you and me. God loves us. God loves everyone in the world. God loves us so much that he sent Jesus, his only son, to this world.

While Jesus was on this earth, he healed the sick; he comforted the sad. He opened blinded eyes. He taught the people many things. We read about this in the Bible.

Jesus wanted us to understand the great love that his father had for you and me. He told this story that explained that love of his father.

A man was happily living in a town with his two sons. He thought all was going well. One day one of the sons rebelled and came to him and said, I do not like this home, I want my own way and I am leaving. Give me my share of the inheritance.

The father was very sad but he gave him the money and let him go. He wondered if he would ever see the son again.

Why the son was so rebellious. The son went far away and enjoyed himself with his money and his friends. He wasted his money and did many bad things. He thought he was having a very good time until suddenly his money ran out and his friends left him.

Then he was left all alone and he felt very guilty. What should I do? He went to a farmer and the farmer sent him to feed the pigs. He was not given enough to eat. He was so hungry he was eaten the pig's food.

He started to think of all the bad things he had done and how he had mistreated his father. He got more and more miserable.

One day he remembered how loving his father was and how well he had it when he was still at home.

He thought, could I go back to my father after all I have done to him. Would he still love me? I am not worthy to be his son. I would be just a servant in his house if only he would take me in.

Suddenly he got to his feet and started for his father's house. He would see if his father would still love him.

The father had been longing for his son ever since he left. He wondered, would my son ever come back. Then one day he saw someone coming in the distance. Could it be my son? He ran to him with outstretched arms and welcomed him back. He said, this my son was lost but now is found.

We have all been like this son; we have all strayed from our heavenly father. We have wasted the opportunities and all the good things he has given us.

We have done bad things and rebelled against him. Today our heavenly father wants us to come to him. He is waiting for us with outstretched arms.

Do you realize the love that Jesus has for us? After he had been teaching on the earth for three years, he allowed wicked men to nail him to the cross.

He suffered pain and rejection as he gave his life and shed his blood as a sacrifice for the sins of the whole world.

When we come to the father, we ask him to forgive our sins. When he sees we are sorry for our sins, he forgives us and washes away all our sin with his blood that he shed.

What a wonderful experience. Jesus has become our savior. We have been born again and become a new person. Life takes on a new meaning. Jesus has replaced our guilt and fear with joy and happiness. Thank you Lord for being the savior of the lives of others and me.

Prayer To The Lord

My Lord and my God of our Lord Jesus Christ and savior of my soul. Thank you for creating me in your image and likeness. Lord Jesus, save me from all my sins, protect me from all dangers and lead me to salvation. Lord Jesus grant that I may love you more. Lord your love continue to burn in me forever and it never fails.

Father God of our Lord Jesus Christ. I am thanking and expressing my heart to you. Father God I know only in believing in Jesus Christ and his finished work on the cross can save me from my sins.

Father God thank you for your faith and for providing your salvation. Father God I know that I have sinned against you and deserve punishment. Lord my sins have separate me and the relationship I had with my heavenly father. I believe Jesus Christ took the punishment I deserve so that through faith in him I could be forgiven.

I receive your offer of forgiveness and place my trust in you for salvation. I confess with my mouth and believe in my heart that Jesus Christ is Lord.

Father God I accept Jesus Christ as my personal savior! Thank you for your wonderful grace and forgiveness, the gift of eternal life!

Thank you also for hearing my prayer and loving me unconditionally. Please give me strength, wisdom and determination to walk in the center of your will. In the name of Jesus Christ.

A Great Need In The
World Today For Love

1 Corinthians 13:4-7 (NIV) Love is patient and kind. Love is not jealous or boastful or proud or rude. It does not demand its own way. It is not irritable, and keeps no record of being wronged. It does not rejoice about injustice but rejoices whenever the truth wins out. Love never gives up, never loses faith, is always hopeful, and endures through every circumstance.

Love is a beautiful word in any language. What does it bring to mind: affection, care, warmth, kindness, understanding, security, and mother?

Nevertheless, think for yourself, what this beautiful word really means. Do you want to be loved? Do you love?

God is love and his love abiding in your heart, I can help you love and be loved. The source of all love is God.

1 John 4:16 (NIV) We know how much God loves us, and we have put our trust in his love. God is love, and all who live in love live in God, and God lives in them.

No one will ever be truly successful in finding or experiencing love unless he seeks it in and through God. Some of the opposites of love are hatred, mistrust, selfishness, war and many more.

We need only look at many of the conditions prevailing in the world and in many families to understand that there is a desperate need for love.

How about you. Do you feel you are loved? Do you feel an ache in your heart, a loneliness that will not go away because you feel no affection, no warmth? Do you at times feel that no one really cares? Have you grown up with parents who did not really love each or their children?

These feelings are common in today's world where the prevailing attitude seems to be me first. An aching heart is the result of an individual indulging in his own selfish interests.

Love is not a sensual attraction that seeks to gratify its own passion, often at the expense of the other person. The attraction, which some may call love, is selfishness because it seeks its own enjoyment. Love does not promote one's own honor or pleasure.

The difficult things that life brings us are not an indication that God does not love us. God at times allows us to experience difficulty for our good.

A parent with true love does not always give a child what he wants, but rather restrains him for the child's benefit.

Love is self-sacrificing. Ture love seeks the good of others. Love is warm, sympathetic, time, kind and many more. If we really love, we will care for the present and future well-being of those near to us.

A loving husband and father will display his affection for his wife and children. He will gladly give and sacrifice of himself to provide an atmosphere of love and well-being.

A wife and mother who truly love will respect her husband and will instill in her children a sense of respect and love for their parents and for each other. She will gladly provide a haven of security and tranquility for all in the family. Christ exemplified love by his undeserved death on the cross.

If you feel the need of love, if there is an emptiness in your heart you can find true love. You can find this by giving yourself to God. God loves you with a tender, compassion that knows no bounds. He cares for you and wants to share and help you through all the headaches of life.

If you feel alone and think that no one really cares, you can rest assured that the one who gave his son for you do feel all your headache and grief. In your loneliest hours and your most dismal days, he will be there to give you comfort, strength, and direction if you turn to him.

If you do not know how to reach God, just pour out your heart to him and he will hear. If you feel you can hardly trust anyone, not even God, tell him so. Then ask him to show you the way.

If you feel you are a sinner without hope of ever finding forgiveness and love, come to God with all your heart, repenting of and leaving your past sins. He will be your loving father if you come to him with all your heart, and willing to obey in all that he asks of you.

When God forgives and accepts you, you will feel his love and gain a relationship with him that nothing can take away. This relationship will only be broken if we turn away from him.

As you come to know the love of God and lose your love of self, you will find security. The security of knowing you are loved, opens your heart to really care about others. You will no longer be so concerned about how people treat you.

You will find that you are concerned about the needs of your fellowmen and that you have a keen desire to be of service to the God who loves you.

When your affection are turned away from self, God will bless you and open your mind to many truths. The teaching in 1 Corinthian 13 (NIV) Will help you understand this clearly.

God also has a family on earth. He may direct you to his family where you will find those who are serving him and doing his will. Jesus said, in John 13:35 (KJV) By this shall all men know that ye are my disciples, if you have love one to another. This is genuine love that cares, shares and correct.

1 Corinthians 13:11-13 (NIV) When I was a child, I speak and thought and reasoned as a child. But when I grew up, I put away childish things. Now we see things imperfectly as in a cloudy mirror, but then we will see everything with perfect clarity. All that I know now is partial and incomplete, but then I will know everything completely. Just as God now knows me completely. Three things will last forever faith, hope and love, and the greatest of these is love.

Let God lead you as you continue reading. There can be an end to your loneliness and unhappiness. Let God take control of your life. Experience God's love, one of the greatest blessings available to all. May God bless you.

A Prayer To The Lord

Lord fill my heart with your glory and my mouth with your praise, so I can declare your wonderful love, for all to see and hear the great things you have done for me.

Lord, Jesus you have shined your light for me to see through the darkest times in my life; thank you Lord Jesus for making away for me when there seen to be no way.

Lord put your song of praise into my heart; fill it with your compassion of never-ending love and unfailing mercy, this I ask in Jesus name.

Lord Jesus, savior and author of salvation, who have conquered the grave and brought me back to life, by washing me in your blood; The blood that fell from the cross and now flowing through the earth.

Lord Jesus when you rose from the grave, you freed me and made me a new person where your Holy Spirit lives forever within me.

Lord Jesus I must confess that it is hard for me, without you in my life. I know I cannot do it on my own understanding and strength. Lord Jesus I lifted my hands and heart to worship and honor you, because you are true, you are who you say you are, and your words are life for my spirit and soul.

Lord Jesus you reign victorious, now and forever in my heart and lips to praise you. Lord, you are lifted up on high; you are seated in heaven with the father on the mercy seat; raining down your blessing on me where the flood gates of heaven has opened.

Lord Jesus I adore you, you are the king of kings and the Lord of Lords. You are worthy to be praise, Lord God almighty. Lord Jesus who was, is and is to come, with all creation; Holy is your name.

Lord Jesus, the good shepherd who takes care of his sheep's, the deliverer, the true bread of life and savior. Who had taken away my darkness and given me his light.

Lord Jesus you have out stretch your hands and healed me from every sickness and protected me from all evil.

Lord Jesus I want to say thank you Lord. You are my redeemer and my friend. I pray that you will strengthen me, fill me with the power of your Holy Spirit of love, faith, service, patient and endurance to exceed in doing your work first.

Lord Jesus search my mind, heart, spirit and soul, cleanse me Lord from anything and everything that I have not confess and repent of. Lord Jesus I repent and ask for your forgiveness from everything I have done knowingly and unknowingly.

Father God guide me on the right path you have set my feet on to follow you. Father God continue to fill me with the power of your Holy Spirit to use your name in the authority of our Lord Jesus Christ.

Lord Jesus cover and fill me with your spirit to be watchful to the end with perseverance, love, hope, faith and courage.

Lord Jesus I ask you to place your whole Spiritual armor of God protection over me; so I can resist and destroy every Spiritual warfare that comes against me in the Spiritual realm of demonic forces. Lord Jesus I submit my life to you.

Lord let the words that I speak be the words of arrows that being dip in the blood of Jesus to destroy the devil kingdom.

In the name of Jesus Christ, I pray for the strength and the authority to use your name Lord, to overcome the enemies in the unseen world, and the enemies in higher places. In the name of Jesus Christ, I declare and stand in hope and faith.

Lord Jesus cover me with your blood and fill me with the power of your spirit to move in the authority of your Holy Spirit day by day, to do thy will.

Lord Jesus fill me with the spirit of faith and Spiritual maturity to overcome the spirit of fear, unbelief and immaturity.

Lord Jesus fill me with the spirit to pray without ceasing and the spirit to wait on God until he responds.

Lord Jesus fill me with an obedient spirit. Lord Jesus fill me with the words of God, write them in my heart, in my mind and in my spirit.

Father God your words are live, powerful and sharper than any two edged sword. Lord surround me with your spirit of prayer worrier, so I may stay strong in prayer and worship in the spirit. In the name of our Lord Jesus Christ, I declare, receive and pray, Amen.

The Sky

The sky is blue. The water is clear above and below is the limit of life. Togetherness makes us whole, united we stand divided we fall.

The light of joy has filled the soul of everything seen and unseen. Love is young and it will never get old.

We are all traveling on a bumpy road to stay awake. Looking at the signs. Paying attention, when to go and when to stop.

There are no short cuts to get true life. Only with the wisdom from the wise. Do not be angry at life. It is not life that is frustrating you and me. it is you and me who are not listening to life.

Hoping for the best. Holding onto faith in God as my strength and my guide. As I walk through the narrow gate, where my father awaits.

Light shining, music playing. Joy of tears has fallen from my eyes, to an awaken heart that's always filled with light. Life is a dance, a song, a celebration in every breath we take.

A journey of life was not in vain. However, a life to gain. Thank you Lord for the ride on the train.

The sky is blue. The water is clear. A grateful heart is one that cares. Where there is joy, there is no more pain. Your joy is my strength Lord, your Love will never change, but it will stay the same.

A Prayer To Circumcise The Heart With The Light Of Jesus

Father God in the name of Jesus I pray that your words will be a light for my heart, my eyes and a lamp for my feet.

Lord Jesus circumcises my heart, my spirit, my mind and my soul to be clean and pure; Lord Jesus circumcises the darkness, the UN forgiveness and all unclean spirits that is in me, around me and against me, that I had adopted from the world; the things I said and done in my past.

Father God in the name of Jesus Christ I pray them out, I also pray out every and anything that came thought, on both my mom and Dad side of the family tree.

Lord Jesus I pray that you will forgive and wash my first family members with your blood and break the chains of captivity from there past lives that may pass on to me.

Lord Jesus I pray that you will close all the doors they had opened and any contracts they had signed will the devil.

Lord Jesus I pray that all, or any relationship, contact, contract and dealing; that any of my first family members had with the devil, are now broken and destroy with fire and blood from our Lord Jesus Christ.

Furthermore, anything they had done knowingly and unknowingly. The things that had nothing to do with the will you had for them; in Jesus name, I pray that you will forgive them and have mercy on them Lord.

In the name of Jesus Christ, I plead your blood over my life, and the lives of my past, present and future family.

Lord Jesus cover us today with your blood and put a seal of protection on us, so that any weapons that comes or form against my family and I shall not prosper.

Lord Jesus I pray that any tongue that speak against my family and I shall not prosper. In Jesus name, I pray.

Lord Jesus draw me into your light, fill me with the spirit of virtue, the spirit of hope and faith for my spirit in Jesus name I pray and receive.

Lord Jesus echo your mercy of love and forgiveness into my heart, spirit, mind and soul in the name of Jesus I ask.

Lord Jesus whisper your love into my heart, fill it with your comforting presence of peace, awaken it, in me, over me, around me and through me; that I may feel your comfort and joy in everything I do and say.

Thank you Lord Jesus, I raise my hands to heaven to praise, to honor and to worship you in thanksgiving, and for the breath of life you breathe in me.

Lord Jesus your name is bless above all names, all the glory, all the honor and all the praise is your now and forever;

My heart rejoices with an everlasting beat of love and gratitude for you Lord. Thank you heavenly father.

Lord Jesus worthy is your name, worthy to be praise. Lord your presence has helped me in my time of need and it has guided me in my time of trouble.

Lord Jesus I know your touch will restore and heal me with the presence of your unfailing love. I am heal by your stripes Lord Jesus. Thank you for healing me.

My blessed redeemer Lord and friend. Lord Jesus you were there with me to revive my soul and spirit when I called you.

Lord Jesus, in your refuge and strength you have covered me in the shadow of your wings and filled me with the presence of your love.

Lord Jesus you have quench my thirst with your love; the love that were shed on the cross, and with your blood that is now flowing into my veins with peace.

Lord, you have feed my soul with your presence of peace. Lord Jesus savior for my soul, my spirit praises you with a deep cry of joy.

I am empty of myself and full of you Lord Jesus; you are my inheritance and my storehouse. In you, Lord Jesus is where my strength and light comes from.

Lord Jesus you are my counselor, my wonderful counselor, redeemer and friend; in you I put my hope, my trust and my faith.

Yes In you Lord Jesus because in you I have found eternal life.

Lord Jesus set my eyes on you, therefore I can see everyone the way you see them and the way you see everything.

Lord your presence has melted every unseen spirits and power that came against me, the spirits that are not from you. Thank you Lord. This I pray declare and receive in the name of Jesus Christ, Amen.

The Lost World

I had been lost into the outer world. Nevertheless, now I have been found into the inner world. There are two or many worlds. There are two side to everything, light and darkness good and evil.

Moreover, both sides spin as the earth spins. Likewise knowing one but not the other. Only what has been taught, walking into the light as we stumble.

Seeing the truth as we walk into the darkness. I can only see the stars when it is dark. A Certain darkness is needed to see the stars.

However many eyes are open and many mouth are shut. What a life and a puzzle to solve. Likewise going with time waiting on the line, for a turn and a chance.

A world created in one by one. Nevertheless, divided into two. It is like a coin with two sides, head and tail, but it is the same coin. A make belief system of illusion, appear to take control. Then speculation began to pop up from the ones who do not know where they are going but they call them self-leaders.

We had been lost in a world of illusion. However, there are hope for us to be found in the truth and the word of God. I saw a ladder: and a voice said to me, freedom is like a ladder, one side of the ladder reaches hell, and the other side touches heaven.

It is the same ladder; the choice is yours; Life or death, blessing or curse you choose.

I chose life and my fear ended. I had to find my balance knowing I cannot take two-step at a time; I cannot be in two places at the same time.

No one else can destroy me except me; no one else can save me, but only the one who created you and me. Indeed, it is still our choice to make.

I will not live in the world that Judas created for himself; but I will live in the world that the God of our Lord Jesus Christ have created for me.

The lost world of opinion about its own self. I came into the world, but I am not of it. Last but not least you and me are the salt of the earth.

Prayer To The Lord

Lord Jesus thank you for the breath of life and for your undying and unfailing love. I just want to say thank you Lord for loving me and for having mercy on me, and for everyone who came to you and believe in your holy name.

Lord Jesus thank you for your unshakeable, unfailing, unchangeable and untouchable love, you have filled and covered me with.

Lord your love has embraced me with a seal that cannot be broken or undone. Lord Jesus fill me with your presence of love and make me aware that you are here.

Lord Jesus fill my mind with your spirit of power, cover my head with the helmet of salvation to stay strong with a sounded mind. Lord Jesus I bow and humble myself to worship you in truth and in spirit. Lord Jesus let your Holy Spirit arise within me, with power to move in your name.

Lord Jesus send your spirit before me, guide me in everything I may do and protect me in the places I may go to. Lord Jesus protect me from the evil one.

Lord Jesus put your light around me. Let your spirit of power guide me, and shine your light for my feet so I may not stumble and fall into temptation. Lord Jesus I pray for the spirit of truth, to declare all the things I can do to bring glory to your name.

Lord I pray that every seed that you have given me to sow will reap the harvest, to bring glory and many people to you, in Jesus name I pray.

Father God I kneel and bow down at the foot of the cross of Jesus Christ, where your mercy and love has cleansed and freed me with the blood from the lamb- (Jesus). This I pray, declare and receive in the name of our Lord and savior Jesus Christ. Amen.

Led By The Spirit Or The Flesh

There are two strong forces in our lives constantly fighting each other, that is why we are not free to carry out our good intentions. We are constantly fighting a battle. The battle we are fighting is the desire of what the flesh want. We are in a battlefield of the mind.

The flesh sets its desire against the spirit, and the spirit against the flesh. We are not fighting against flesh and blood we are also fighting against spiritual being in the heavenly places. The devil who is the prince of the power of the air.

A dark veil is covering many of our face and hearts from seeing who we really are. There is a battle going on between good and evil. From the beginning of time there been a battle going on, between flesh vs spirit, Evil vs good.

In the beginning God created everything including you and me, man and woman in his image and his likeness; God breath the breathe of life into the first man Adam.

Moreover, Adam became a living being in the spirit in the Garden of Eden and had a relationship with his creator (God).

Nevertheless, God also created a helper for Adam a woman her name is eve. God has given Adam and Eve a commanded what they should do and what not to do, what to eat and what not to eat.

Adam and Eve decided to listen to the flesh and went their own way. They were deceived by the devil that came to them in the form of a serpent, because they disobeyed God.

When God created man, he created him to have a relationship with him; man was created to live forever. When man had disobeyed God, God had to banish him from the Garden of Eden. Therefore, they can return to him as he created them.

God had given a man by the name of Moses his law and commandments to give to his people to follow, and to show them what they are doing, they should not be doing.

The law was given to Moses by God alongside the promise to show people their sins. The law was designed to last only until the coming of the child who was promise through angels to Moses.

Indeed God had a plan for man to return to him; so God decided to send his only son into the world of darkness as a light and a sheep for you and me to fine our way back to him.

Galatians 3:22 (NIV) But the Scriptures declare that we are all prisoners of sin, so we receive God promise of freedom only by believing in Jesus Christ.

To be led by the spirit of God of our Lord Jesus Christ. You have to be born again in the spirt; you need to ask Jesus to renew you and make you new again.

To be led by the spirit of God we have to ask Jesus to come into our heart and spirit, and to be our Lord and savior of our lives.

Moreover, by confessing with our mouth and believing in our heart, that Jesus is Lord and that God has sent him to die for our sins; the sin that came from our first parents, Adam and eve.

Jesus said that he is the way the truth and the life no one comes to the father but by him first. All who are not led by the of God are led by the flesh or some others spirit. Moreover, if you want to be born again in the spirit of God spiritual family;

All you need to do is confess with your mouth and believe in your heart that Jesus is Lord. Ask Jesus to come into your life and fill you with his Holy Spirit.

Galatian 3: 23-26 (NIV) Before the way of faith in Christ was available to us, we were placed under guard by the law. We were kept in protective custody, so to speak, until the way of faith was revealed.

Let me put it another way. The law was our guardian until Christ came; it protected us until we could be made right with God through faith. And now that the way of faith has come, we no longer need the law as our guardian. For we are all children of God through faith in Christ Jesus.

2 Corinthians 4:3 (NIV) If the good news we preach is hidden behind a veil, it is hidden only from people who are perishing. Satan, who is the god of this world, has blinded the minds of those who do not believe.

They are unable to see the glorious light of the good news. They do not understand this message about the glory of Christ, who is the exact likeness of God.

We are God's ambassadors; we are God's sons and daughters. We are all made in the image and likeness of God. The God of our Lord Jesus Christ has given you and me a new way to live.

Galatians 5:16-18 (NIV) So I say let the Holy Spirit guide your lives. Then you won't be doing what your sinful nature craves. The sinful nature wants to do evil, which is just the opposite of what the spirit wants.

And the spirit gives us desires that are the opposite of what the sinful nature desire. These two forces are constantly fighting each other, so you are not free to carry out your good intention.

But when you are directed by the spirit, you are not under obligation to the law of Moses.

Ephesian 5:15 (NIV) So be careful how you live. Do not live like fools, but like those who are wise. Make the most of every opportunity in these evil days. Do not act thoughtlessly, but understand what the Lord wants you to do.

Jesus said ask and you shall receive, he also said keep on asking in his name, the name the father have given him. There is no greater love than one to lay down his life for a friend. What a friend we have in Jesus. Do not quit but believe and put your trust and faith in God and also Jesus.

Joshua 1:9 (NIV) This is my command; be strong and courageous! Do not be afraid or discouraged. For the Lord your God is with you wherever you go.

Many today believe that all churches are right. In other words, it does not really matter which church one goes to.

They say, God has saved people in all churches. It is up to the individual in each church to be sincere in his or her worship and accept Jesus Christ as his and her personal savior.

Once you were dead because of your disobedience and your many sins. You used to live in sin, just like the rest of the world, obeying the devil- the commander of the power in the unseen world. He is the spirit at work in the hearts of those who refuse to obey God.

Ephesians 2:3-5 (NIV) All of us used to live that way, following the passionate desires and inclination of our sinful nature. By our very nature, we were subject to God's anger, just like everyone else.

I would like to ask each reader to be open minded. In Hebrews 3:15 (NIV) Today when you hear his voice, don't harden your hearts, as Israel did when they rebelled.

Prayer To The Lord For Direction

Lord of our father in heaven; thank you for the breathe of life and your unfailing love in your son Jesus the Christ.

Lord Jesus my cry and my desire is to be with you wherever you are. Lord in my ups and down I know you are right here with me.

Lord Jesus in your words, you promise that you will never leave me or forsaken me. Lord you promise you will be with me until the end of time.

Lord Jesus the promise you made and your love for me on the cross, have showed me, how much you love and care for me;

Lord Jesus when you stretch your hands on the cross for me. That is how much I know you love and cared for me; and I can live and still believe in your name all the days of my life.

Lord, you are the Holy and the truth in what you had said and done in your words. The promises you made through your son Jesus father God.

Lord Jesus fill my heart with the sound and vibration of your trumpet of love in the name of Jesus Christ I pray.

Lord, you hold everything in your hands, the hands you created everything with, your love endure forever.

Lord you are the one and only God who had never changes, but remain the same. Lord Jesus I pray for your direction and your guidance.

Lord and my God, you are the same yesterday, today and forever more. You are the alpha and the Omega. Lord Jesus your name are the name above all name, you are the Holy and righteous one.

Lord Jesus fill me with your spirit of light and remind me of who I am in you and who you are in me. Lord Jesus, you said, you are the vines and I am the branches.

Lord your love endures forever, all the glory, the honor and praise is your now and forever. In the name of Jesus I worship and honor, you father God.

My hope is in you Lord, my hope is built on nothing else than you Lord Jesus. All the power is your, you are the king of the heavens and the earth. You are worthy to be praise with honor, glory and truth.

Lord Jesus cover and clothed me with your Spiritual garments and wash me with the blood of Jesus; so I can live a faithful and obedience life.

Lord Jesus I pray and ask you to fill me with your spirit to repent and the spirit to confess all the things I did, doing and may do.

Father God I confess and believe in my heart that Jesus is Lord. Lord fill me with the spirit of self-control and integrity. Lord strengthen me in my walk with you in the mighty name of Jesus.

Lord Jesus continue to bless my feet to walk on soiled ground and on a straight path to you. Lord Jesus shine your light before and behind me as a shield of protection.

You are my rock and my light Lord, you are the way the truth and the life. Lord Jesus shine your light for my feet so I may not stumble and fall into temptation; but to rise above all the things that is not from you.

Lord Jesus empty me from all of me and fill me with all of you, this I pray and ask in the name of Jesus Christ.

Lord let your Spirit of love flow in me like rivers of living water of joy, peace, victory and love.

The greatest of all is love, your love Jesus. In the name of Jesus, I pray, I declare and receive your blessing, your love, and your guidance Lord Jesus. Amen.

A Neighbor And Friend

In the world today, as you can see many of us are trying to find God in our complicated countries, cities, states and neighborhoods.

We are living in a time where our countries, cities, states and neighborhoods are being under attack and being taken over and run by dark forces.

Do not let these words scare you, but it is true: the enemy knows your neighborhood.

In many countries and neighborhoods, God is slowly being taken out of everything; in our schools in our national anthem, the list goes on.

Do we serve a placeless God? On the other hand, do we serve a God who can be found in our countries, cities, and neighborhood even in the dark, gritty, complicated corners and alleys?

Yes, we can, God is everywhere. The enemy knows that. That is why he is trying to take God out of everything. The enemy may try to take God out of everything, but do not let him take God and the love of Jesus out of you. Do not believe the lies the enemy is saying to you.

There is hope; greater is he that is in you is greater than he that lives in the world. We are more than conqueror; we are sons and daughters of a king.

We need to be praying more for our countries and in all the areas of our neighborhoods and communities were our children's live and where they are playing. The devil is roaming all around looking to see who he can devourer.

The devil is a liar and a thief; he has been trying so hard from the beginning of time to take over every area of our lives by putting strong holds in the places we are living.

Let us come together in prayers and pray out the enemy that is polluting our neighborhood and country's; we need to work together not against each other.

In prayer, we can move anything that comes against us. In spirit and in truth, in the name of our Lord Jesus Christ we have the power to do all things big and small.

Moreover, let us speak good things about our neighbor's and others; remember the words that comes out of our mouth can give life and it can bring death also.

However many of us may not know, or be fully aware of the work we are doing for the enemy without knowing. The devil is a liar and a thief. You and I are made in the image and likeness of God through our Lord Jesus Christ. Therefore, we should be working for God and not for the devil. The devil is still rebelling against God and he is trying to use you and me so that he can get back at God.

Do not fall for the lies from the devil; let us rise above his lies by using the name, words and power of our Lord Jesus. There is power in the name of Jesus; we are all covered with his blood.

Do not take revenge and repay evil to anyone who may have done you wrong or been unfair to you; let us pray, let us put our trust and let us wait on the Lord he will deliver you and me.

Proverbs 10:11 (NIV) The words of the godly are a life giving fountain, the words of the wicked conceals violent intention.

Follow the path of righteousness; proverbs 11:5 (NIV) The righteousness of the perfect shall direct his way; but the wicked shall fall by his own wickedness.

The name of the Lord is a strong tower; the righteous man runs into it and is safe.

God is our shield and refuge; every word of God proves true; he is a shield to those who take refuge in him.

Prayer for our Neighborhood

Lord Jesus, all powerful, mighty and unchangeable God, who are the same from the beginning of time until the end of age.

Father God I pray and ask in the name of our Lord Jesus, to watch over and bless the neighborhood I am living in; Lord continue bless the country, the state and the communities I grow up in.

Lord Jesus continue to bless the children in the world, put your hands of protection over them, and open the right doors for them so they can walk through to see you.

Lord Jesus protect them from the evil one and his followers. Father God continue to bless all the mothers and the fathers on the earth we are living in; Lord Jesus give them the wisdom and understanding to bring up their children in the way to know you when they are young in mind.

Lord Jesus I pray that you will put the right people in our neighborhoods, communities, country and state.

Lord Jesus I pray that you will take out the wrong people and put the right people in our lives; in Jesus name I pray and ask.

Lord Jesus I pray that you will strengthen the churches in our neighborhoods, our communities, our country and the people who is playing church.

Father God I pray in the name of Jesus that you will fill us with the Holy Spirit and wash us with your blood.

Lord Jesus above all powers, above all kings and kingdoms; you are above all. There is nothing worth more than you Lord.

The power of your name is a protection and shield for us to go through this life. Lord Jesus send your spirit of light to shine out all the darkness, all the evil spirits and all the crimes that is happening in our neighborhoods.

Lord Jesus I pray out everyone and everything that is not from you, and not helping our people; in our neighborhoods and communities to grow Spiritual. Lord I pray and ask in the name of Jesus for the spirit of unity, peace, joy, happiness, comfort, power and light; to fill our lives, our homes, our country, our neighborhoods, our communities and our schools so we can walk and shine in your name.

Lord Jesus cover our neighborhoods with the shadow of your wings and with your amazing grace. Lord fill our neighborhoods with your spirit of faith, love, hope, courage, peace and unity in the name of Jesus I pray.

Lord Jesus fill our neighborhoods with your sweet sound of hope, spirit and truth. Lord Jesus send your good shepherd to our lost sheep.

Farther God in the name of Jesus I ask you to wash our neighborhoods with the precious blood of your beloved son Jesus.

Lord Jesus feed our neighborhoods with the bread of life and the spirit of living water. In the name of Jesus Christ, I pray and declare for you to wash our neighborhoods with your blood and fill it with your grace and salvation. In the name of Jesus, I pray, believe and declare. Amen.

Life Worth Living In A Restless World

This world is a restless place. We see people dashing about trying to find meaning in activity. Many dedicate themselves to gather riches. While others want all the pleasure of the sensual life, still others want more leisure and arrange to work less and play more. Yet their spirits are not satisfied. Pleasures and possessions eventually lose their attractiveness.

Every new diversion are fill in for a time but quickly loses its appeal. Something seems to be missing. We all have our share of disappointment. Physical defects limit our activities. Family members need constant care.

We feel trapped in a job or vocation because we lack expertise to take up other work. We spend money and go into debt hoping the next purchase will make tolerable.

Example) Our marriage and others relationship has not proved to be what we had hoped. In vain, we look for fulfillment and purpose.

Is that all there is to life? Should there not be something meaningful to give us satisfaction, something more permanent? Surely, there is a solution.

What is life? Life is a precious span of time allotted by the creator. The bible says it is like a shadow.

1 chronicles 29:15 (NIV) We are here for only a moment, visitors and strangers in the land as our ancestors were before us. Our days on earth are like a passing shadow, gone so soon without a trace.

1 peter 1:24-25 (NIV) As the scriptures say, people are like grass; their beauty is like a flower in the field. The grass withers and the flower fades.

Nevertheless, the word of the Lord remains forever. In addition, that word is God news that was preached to you.

James 4:14 (NIV) How do you know what your life will be like tomorrow? Your life is like the morning fog, it is here a little while, and then it is gone.

While we are young, we see life extending for years. As we get older, time seem to speed up. We cannot accomplish what we had hoped for earlier. We are disappointed by a variety of hindrances that cramp our lifestyle.

What is the problem?

What contributes to the discontent of our spirit? Life is an opportunity but also a responsibility. We are unhappy whenever we violate the good we know we should do.

Sin against our fellow man brings about uneasiness and guilt. Sin against ourselves has its destructive effects on our peace of mind. We feel responsible for our deeds.

Most people have a sort of intuition that life figures into a larger picture than the few short years on earth.

For many this means they need to recognize a higher spiritual power, a higher purpose at work in the universe. They may not always know who or what that is.

Often people are dissatisfied with life because they fail to see God's perspective. They are ignorant of God's will and purpose for man, sometimes willingly so.

Many fail to envision the eternal bliss of the faithful and they would rather ignore the final reaping of the wicked and godless.

Romans 6:23 (NIV) For the wages of sin is death, but the free gift of God is eternal life through Christ Jesus our Lord and savior.

The abundant life is available to all.

Jesus say in John 16:24 (NIV) You haven't done this before. Ask using my name, and you will receive, and you will have abundant joy.

The joy that Jesus gives is not easily removed from a Christian's heart or any heart he visits. At times, we are heavy-hearted because of temptations. The joy that is a fruit of the Holy Spirit's presence within runs deeper than those weights.

It may not be the bubbling, light feeling but simply a calm trust in the Lord that allows us to stand unwavering in trial and unconquered by the storm. Some may tell you that the Christian way is too restrictive to be enjoyed.

They might think that in order to be happy you must be able to do as you please. Just try the Lord! You will find it is a pleasure to serve the one who died for you.

It will become clear to you that the person who serves himself is really the one in bondage and the servant of Christ is the free man.

The true fulfillment is not found in following trends and fashions or patterning our lives to impress others. That kind of living becomes a compelling force and leads to bondage.

When we are humble, we are free. Free to be ourselves. Free to rest our minds from thoughts of what others are thinking of us.

Jesus offers life worth living; in Matthew 11:28 (NIV) Than Jesus said, come to me, all of you who are weary and carry heavy burdens, and I will give you rest.

Here the son of God, Jesus Christ, offers rest to all who have burdens to bear, whose life-load seem more than they can carry, whose life is unfulfilled, whose life lacks purpose. Come to the Lord and give him your load of your sin, your load of dissatisfaction. Admit your inability to handle life's problems. Turn from what you know to be wrong in your life. Give your life over to Jesus. Trust him to take you by the hand and lead you.

Once you realize you need help in your life, you can come to Jesus and receive that help. As long as you feel independent and self-sufficient; He can do nothing for you. When you yield yourself to his care, there is hope for you.

Jesus Christ can fill the deepest longing of your soul. Yield your life and your will to him. As you, ask him to fill you with his abundance life in all its fullness will be yours.

A Prayer For Grace

Father God in the name of Jesus Christ, I pray in the spirit for your grace and your spirit of truth. In the name of Jesus, I lift my hands to the heavens with praises and thanksgiving; I welcome you Lord Jesus with open heart, worship and praises.

Lord I pray for grace, mercy, guidance and love for our generation today and the generation to come, in the name of Jesus I pray.

Lord Jesus I pray for grace for the lost, the blind and the deaf. Lord may your light shine in our hearts to see and to do your will.

Lord fill our hearts with your spirit to move in power, hope and faith in Jesus name.

Lord let your river of love flow in our heart, mind, body and spirit with your light of salvation. Lord Jesus you are the Lamb of God who taken away the sins of the world and brought everlasting light to our hearts.

Lord, I may not know all the plans you have for my life; but I know all will work out for good to bring glory to your name.

Lord fill me with your love and the spirit that raise Jesus from the grave.

Lord Jesus I know at the cross where your blood were shed for me; there is a promise you made, that promise is a seal and anchor written with your blood of victory on my heart.

Lord Jesus your words are unshakeable, unstoppable, unfailing and lovable, even when the heavens and the earth have passed away, your words remain the same.

All my hope is in your name Lord, because there is power in the name of Jesus. Lord Jesus your tenderness of your love, your mercy and your words has brought me comfort and answers to who I am in you.

Lord I may not be perfect in the eyes of the people who are of the world. I am perfect in your eyes, because you made me in your image and likeness.

Thank you Lord Jesus, your love has given me the sweetest comfort, from your presence of peace, to bring glory to your name.

Lord Jesus fill us with your joy of your salvation, so we could become more aware of your glory and your presence victory.

To experience your goodness and love Lord, in all the places we may go and all the things we may do and say; in Jesus name, I pray. Amen.

Lord Jesus I know my soul is secure because of your promise you had made. Lord, I will never stop worshipping you, because you love me and your love never fails.

In the name of Jesus Christ, I pray for the grace for the ruins to come alive in the presence of your beautiful name.

Lord Jesus I pray that we will find refuge, love, peace, joy, grace and mercy on our journey of life In Jesus mighty name. This I pray and I declare and believe, in the name of Jesus Christ. Amen.

The Answer To Our Problems

Psalms 23:2-3 (KJV) He maketh me to lie down in green pastures; he leadeth me beside the still waters. He restoreth my soul; he leadeth me in the paths of righteousness for his name's sake.

Do you have feeling of loneliness or a sense of guilt and fear deep inside your heart? Do you wonder about the purpose of life? Many people are trying to find the answer to those feeling. You may find entertainments or other activities that may relieve you of these feelings for a short time, then they return, perhaps stronger than ever before.

In the beginning, God's creation was perfect. Man had no problem until the devil came and enticed him to disobey God. He fell into sin and he was no longer perfect. Ever since that time all humanity has been sinful.

Can you relate to this fall? When you were a child, God was not keeping track of your sins. However, was forgiving you and me for Jesus' sake.

As you and me matured these things began to change, you and me started to have guilty feeling. What happen? God was letting us feel the guilt of our sins. No longer was the blood of Jesus covering our sins. God was saying, you are now responsible for what you are doing." If you have not accepted Jesus as your savior, you are still carrying a burden of guilt.

What can you do to change these feeling of guilt? You cannot pay for your sins no matter how much good deeds you do. In God's eyes, you are still a sinner. God cannot tolerate sin. Sin separates us from God.

Isaiah 59:2 (NIV) It is your sins that have cut you off from God. Because of sins, he has turned away and will not listen anymore.

Now here is the beautiful and simple plan God has to help you and me. Jesus, God sinless and perfect son came to bring this plan. He took our sins upon himself and died on the cross, paying the price that was demanded for our sins.

Through the death and resurrection of Jesus, we can have salvation today. Jesus invites you and me to come to him with the burden of sin.

God wants to help you and me. He will forgive you and me when we are willing to admit that we are sinner and call on him to help. Not all our efforts and good intention can cleanse us from sin.

There is only one way you can be cleansed from your sins and that is by having the blood of Jesus Christ applied to your heart.

When the blood of Christ has cleansed you, you will realize that you could not change your life by your own power. You must believe that God has the wisdom and keeping power for your life.

If you come to God with all your heart, forsake your sins and follow in obedience, he will do what is best for you.

This is faith-trusting God completely with your life. Once you have given all to God, the peace that you receive in your heart will be the evidence that he has forgiven you.

The forgiveness you receive from God will make you free; free with the sweet confidence that now you are a child of God, made perfect by the blood of Jesus Christ. A new purpose is born that will enable you and me to overcome feeling of fear and emptiness.

Matthew 6:34 (NIV) So don't worry about tomorrow, for tomorrow will bring its own worries. Today's trouble is enough for today.

John 3:16 (NIV) For God so loved the world so much that he gave his one and only son, so that everyone who believes in him will not perish but have eternal life.

John 14:15 (NIV) If you love me, obey my commandments.

A Prayer To The Lord

Father God of our Lord Jesus Christ, I thank you for the sky as my roof over my head and the earth as my bed to rest my head. Your love is so amazing father God; you gave your one and only son Jesus Christ as a ransom for others and me. Thank you Lord Jesus.

Lord Jesus your love is far beyond measures, far beyond words can express. Lord Jesus I will boast in your name and the love you have resurrected within me; I will boast to the world with a humble spirit until the end of my life on earth.

Thank you Lord, your love is amazing and full of life and peace. At the cross Lord Jesus I come for you to wash me and fill me with your glory, your love, your spirit, your peace, your wisdom and your understanding.

Lord Jesus your name is Holy and your words is life for my soul and spirit. Lord your love has captured my heart and has pierced it with your presences.

Lord Jesus anoints my head with your blood, seal my spirit with the joy of your salvation and lead my feet with your spirit of light and truth where you are.

Lord Jesus by your wounds I am healed and by your blood and grace I am saved.

Lord continue to bless and fill my heart to declare who you are with a bold and a humble spirit; in the mighty and holy name of Jesus Christ. These I pray, declare, believe and receive, in Jesus name, Amen.

How To Get Out Of Prison

John 8:36 (KJV) If the son therefore shall make you free, ye shall be free indeed.

Everyone wants to be free. The freedoms of speech, thought, religion, and press are basic to many societies in the world today. Society has found it necessary to restrict the freedom of lawbreakers, to allow others the enjoyment of their rightful freedom.

That is why prison exists. People who break the laws of the land may well find themselves in a literal prison.

Example there is many ways we can create, be or live in a prison; many of us are prisoner of ourselves.

Are people really free while enjoying the liberties mentioned, or are many of them in a different kind of prison? The Bible teaches us that people may be in bondage even while they are seeking liberty.

A person who tells one lie finds him and her in bondage to that lie, and is often led to lie again to cover the first untruth.

People who take up smoking, drinking, or drugs find out later, when they wish to quit, that they are unable to do so. Many others have broken marriage vows for the sake of pleasure and found themselves with neither pleasure nor family.

These are examples of the bondage that sin brings. Bondage to sin is universal and everyone is born in sin. The Bible tells us in Romans 3:23 (KJV) For all have sinned, and come short of the glory of God.

Romans 6:16 (NIV) Don't you realize that you become the slave of whatever you choose to obey. You can be a slave to sin, which leads to death, or you can choose to obey God, which leads to righteous living.

While we are still in our sins, we are in a spiritual prison. How can we be delivered? True freedom, true happiness, freedom from fear, freedom from guilt and condemnation, can come only when we are at peace with God and our lives are in agreement with his will.

Likewise, bondage on the other hand, is the result of reaching out for Satan's false promise of liberty. Let us turn to the words of our savior, Jesus Christ:

Luke 4:18 (KJV) The spirit of the Lord is upon me, because he hath anointed me to preach the gospel to the poor; he hath sent me to heal the brokenhearted, to preach deliverance to the captives, and recovering of sight to the blind, to set at liberty them that are bruised.

To be delivered from sin, we must first admit that we are sinners and in bondage. We must repent of our sins. Repentance includes sorrow for our and turning away from sin. This may seem difficult or nearly impossible to some.

If we make an honest effort, and call on God for help and for forgiveness of sin, the Lord will lead us step by step to a conversion of the heart.

We must accept deliverance and forgiveness by the blood of Jesus through faith. We read in the Bible, Colossians 1:4 (KJV) In whom

Jesus we have redemption through his blood, even the forgiveness of sins.

who purchased our freedom and forgave our sins.

Romans 3:24-25 (NIV) Yet God, with underserved kindness, declares that we are righteous. He did this through Christ Jesus when he freed us from the penalty for our sins.

For God presented Jesus as the sacrifice for sin. People are made right with God when they believe that Jesus sacrifice his life, shedding his blood. This sacrifice shows that God was being fair when he help back and did not punish those who sinned in times past.

Romans 5:1 (NIV) Therefore, since we have been made right in God's sight by faith, we have peace with God because of what Jesus Christ our Lord has done for us.

Acts 3:19 (NIV) Now repent of your sins and turn to God, so that your sins may be wiped away.

John 3:3 (NIV) Jesus replied, I tell you the truth, unless you are born again, you cannot see the kingdom of God.

What are the effects of this spiritual freedom? When a person is truly, born again as described above, his sins are washed away, and he has a free conscience.

He now has power over sinful desires. Instead of yielding to temptation, he now is able to resist the desires of the flesh. He is living a new life in Christ and his aims are different.

Instead of living only to please himself he now seeks to please God and help others. His speech and use of time are different. He rejoices in the challenges of a life that is now filled with purpose and direction.

Best of all, this freedom brings an assurance of eternal life in heaven. Even in the confines of a natural prison, this freedom of spirit and heart can be a reality.

We read, in 2 Corinthians 5:17 (KJV) Therefore if any man be in Christ, he is a new creature: old things are passed away; behold, all things are become new.

Galatians 5:13 (NIV) For you have been called to live in freedom, my brothers and sisters. But don't use your freedom to satisfy your sinful nature. Instead, use your freedom to serve one another in love.

A Prayer Forgive Me

Lord Jesus thank you for dying on the cross for my sins. Thank you Lord for your mercy and your grace.

Father God I ask in the name of your son Jesus Christ to forgive me as, I forgive others and those who has trespass against me and those I have trespassed against.

Lord Jesus I forgive myself for all the things I had said and done to myself knowingly and unknowingly, from my past and through my days and years on this earth.

Lord I release myself from every and anything that is holding me back from doing the things you have called me to do on this earth. In the name of Jesus, I pray. Amen.

Father God let your light shine in me, and in every area of my life washing my heart, my spirit and my soul with the blood from Jesus.

I am free, I am blessed, I am protected and I am saved in the name and blood of Jesus. I now believe in the name of Jesus and I welcome him into my heart as Lord and savior.

Lord Jesus arise in me with power, love and the desire to worship you in truth and in Spirit. Lord Jesus let your light shine within my spirit, mind and soul.

Lord shine out every and anything that is hiding and causing me to stumble.

Father God of our Lord Jesus Christ I pray for you to break the yoke of slavery from my neck and give me the strength to walk with my head held high. In the name of Jesus, I pray, I declare, I believe and I receive the power to do all things. In the mighty name of Jesus. Amen.

Lack Of Knowledge

Hosea 4:6 (NIV) My people are being destroyed because they do not know me. Since you priests refuse to know me, I refuse to recognize you as my priests. Since you have forgotten the laws of your God, I will forget to bless your children.

It is becoming increasingly more difficult to distinguish truth from lies, light from dark and good from evil; but I tell you there are one way, one answer, Jesus Christ the messiah and redeemer.

He has every answers and he hold all the keys. Jesus said, I am the way the truth and the life. No one comes to the father or enter his kingdom, except through him. Jesus is the ladder and the door. Jesus also said I am the shepherd and my sheep know my voice and they follow me.

Moreover follow Jesus and only Jesus, do not listen to the voice of another. We need to get back to the voice of God through his written word to us and stop listening to the voices of this world! We want the promise without the precepts!

Those who serve God only in the good times, or only when they need something from him will not endure.

The word of God tells us in Matthew 24:11-13 (NIV) And many false prophets will appear and will deceive many people. Sin will be rampant everywhere, and the love of many will grow cold. Nevertheless, the one who endures to the end will be saved. And the good news about the kingdom will be preached throughout the whole world, so that all nations will hear it; and then the end will come.

A Prayer To The Lord

Lord cover me with favor as a shield. Lord let the words of my mouth and the mediation of my heart be acceptable in your sight, o Lord, my rock and redeemer.

Father God of our Lord Jesus Christ. Thank you for loving me, as I am; thank you Lord for your mercy, your love and your grace.

I am here to worship you Lord. You are an amazing God, whose words and love never fails. However, remain the same; Likewise shining out every darkness from within out.

There is no other father that can compare to the love and peace I have found in you Lord.

Lord Jesus I have heard so many stories about who you are and whom you are not.

Father God the spirit you breathe within me knows who you are and what you can do. Lord Jesus my heart never denied who you are, but express how perfect you are in all of your ways.

Lord Jesus your love is deeper than were we can go or imagine. Lord Jesus everything revolves around you, because you are the center of our heart, mind, spirit and soul.

The stone that the builder rejected have now become the head cornerstone, the chief cornerstone. Lord you are the cornerstone the builder has rejected, but still that builder needs that same cornerstone he had rejected, to build on.

Therefore, he and she can have a soiled foundation to live on, so they can survive. In the name of Jesus, I pray. Amen.

Lord Jesus thank you for purchasing my pardon on Calvary with your blood; thank you for dying on the cross for my sins, so I can have life in you.

Lord Jesus your glittering light has crowned my heart with the presence of your endless peace, joy and love.

Lord Jesus I have found you in me with your arms stretch wide open. Lord nothing matters after I felt your comforting hands of love, peace and protection. Lord Jesus I surrender all the things in the world that is and was holding me back from doing what you have called me to do. Lord let your will be done in me.

Lord fill me with thy power and strength to overcome the things in the world. Lord shine your light in me so I can see everyone, I may encounter; Lord Jesus let me see them the way you see them.

Father God I pray and ask you to remove and unseal every strong hold and power, from Satan spirit; away from me and in my pathway of life.

In the name of Jesus Christ, I thank you, I pray, I declare, believe and I receive your blessing. In the name of Jesus, Amen.

Who Are You Following And Listening Too

Your choices determine your future. Our father of our Lord Jesus has given you and me the free will of choices to make. Moreover, he has given you and me life and death, blessing and curse, to choose from. However, he told us to choose life.

Proverbs 18:21 (NIV) The tongue can bring death or life; those who love to talk will reap the consequences.

Furthermore, after the fall of humankind and because of the choice of disobedience with pride, man had made; the whole world of the human race fell and had to pay the price.

In this life on earth we are living, they will always be a price to be paid; to someone or something. What a life, many of us has been thinking. We all need someone, we need each other; we are many parts that came from one body. The body need the head and the hands needs the shoulder.

Indeed, there is still hope for the human race (you and me) in Christ Jesus with hope and faith in God.

Therefore, my question is whom are you following and listening too; not every road is the right road and not every voice you hear will guide you to Jesus.

Likewise not all that glitter is gold. Jesus said I am the way the truth and the life, no one can go to father, but by him first.

To illustrate a little more, Jesus, the light of the world. John 8:12 (NIV) Jesus, spoke to the people once more and said, "I am the light of the world. If you follow me, you won't have to walk in darkness, because you will have the light that leads to life."

The bible tells us that in the last days some will follow deceptive spirits and teaching that comes from demons. Moreover, many people ear will be itching them to hear what they want to here. And not what the God of our Lord Jesus Christ had said.

Therefore, I will say the flesh is weak but your spirit should be willing. Likewise, the spirit of God lives in you and me; because greater is he that live in you and me is greater than the spirit that lives in the world.

The Lord Jesus said man shall not live by bread alone, but by every word that comes from the mouth of God.

Furthermore, you may know the tree by its fruit it bears. Jesus said I am the vine and you are the branches, without Jesus you and me will not bear good fruit.

John 15:5 (NIV) Yes, I am the vine; you are the branches. Those who remain in me, and I in them, will produce much fruit. For apart from me you can do nothing. Do not let you heart be trouble. I do nothing on my own but say only what the father taught me.

John 10:1-5 (NIV) I tell you the truth, anyone who sneaks over the wall of a sheepfold, rather than going through the gate, must surely be a thief and a robber!

But the one who enters through the gate is the shepherd of the sheep. The gatekeeper opens the gate for him, and the sheep recognize his voice and come to him.

He calls his own sheep by name and leads them out. After he has gathered his own flock, he walks ahead of them, and they follow him because they know his voice. They won't follow a stranger; they will run from him because they don't know his voice.

Do you know the voice and direction of the God of our Lord Jesus Christ. The voice of God is in the Holy Bible, the words spoken by our Lord Jesus.

When Moses led the Israelite out of Egypt, it was the voice of God that spoke to Moses; and it was the spirit of God that led them out of Egypt.

The path to life is very narrow and few will find it, my sheep knows my voice and they listen. Broad is the way to destruction. Now look at it this way;

(Awareness) the question many people will ask, well if narrow is the way, them why it is so hard. My reply is I do not think it is hard, I think it is very challenging. When we do not listen to the voice of God.

Indeed many people will respond in many different ways. That is ok; everyone is entitled to his or her own opinions. I am speaking base on what the word of God said.

When God give you a commanded, you should follow it and put your trust in his word. Jesus said I am the way the truth and the life. He also said I will never leave you are forsake you. I am the vine and you are the branches, apart from me, you will bear no fruit. In my father house there are many mansions therefore, I will go and prepare a place for you.

When God spoke to Moses to lead the Israelites out of Egypt, God had a plan for them; to get to the place he had promise for them.

However, when things was getting challenging the Israelites started to complain that it is too hard for them. Likewise, they wanted to go back in to Egypt. They wanted to stay slaves than be free; their faith and trust was in the things of the world, instead of the faith of the God who created the world and everything in it.

God will always make away when there seem to be no way. All we have to do is believe and trust God; God have a plan and hope and a future for all of us, you and me.

Nevertheless, when you choose to follow and go your own way you will find out the hard way; just like some of the people in the bible that went their own way; instead of the way God has showed you and me through his son Jesus Christ.

Matthew 7:13-14 (NIV) You can enter God's kingdom only through the narrow gate. The highway to hell is broad, and its gate is wide for the many who choose that way. But the gateway to life is very narrow and the road is difficult, and only a few ever find it.

Moreover, narrow is the way to help you and me find our way to our Lord Jesus Christ, and it also gives us the strength to grow more from the challenges we face on that journey.

Furthermore, like I said broad is the way to destruction and it can lead you to many things; however I said that to make it clear, because broad is open to everything, but there is consequences for everything in it. Therefore, the choices we make we will have to live with them; and it will determine our future.

Proverb 14:12 (NIV) There is a path before each person that seems right but it ends in death.

Where there is a will there is a way. Jesus is the only way to the father.

Romans 1:20 (NIV) For ever since the world was created, people have seen the earth and sky through everything God made, they can clearly see his invisible qualities- his eternal power and divine nature. So they have no excuse for knowing God.

2 John 1:9 (NIV) Anyone who wanders away from this teaching has no relationship with God. But anyone who remains in the teaching of Christ has a relationship with both the father and the son.

Indeed look at the people in the world, look at how many of us are living our lives; God of our lord Jesus Christ created you and me to obey and have a relationship with him.

Furthermore, Jesus has set an example for you and me to follow, and he has showed us what we should do and how we should live; Jesus said I give you a commandment to love. Moreover, Jesus wants you and me to take refuge in him.

Psalm 118:8-9 (NIV) It is better to take refuge in the Lord than to trust in people. It is better to take refuge in the Lord than to trust in princes.

We should seek the God of our Lord Jesus Christ; the God that created creation, not the others way around. Do not put your hope and trust in man, put your hope, trust and faith in God.

Many people preach the word of God like the Pharisees, and they twist the word of God in many different ways to look good in the eyes of people.

Indeed these people are false and blind guides; they are plants that God did not plant to do his work. Many are called but few are chosen.

These people preach in the flesh and not in the spirit. Therefore, you do not have to worry about anything; because God will take care of you and me.

Matthew 15:13-14 (NIV) Jesus replied, every plant not planted by my heavenly father will be uprooted. So ignore them they are blind guides leading the blind, and if one blind person guides another, they will both fall into a ditch.

We are living in a falling world, a world that been divided; likewise, everyone is a teacher of so kind.

Matthew 23:2-4 (NIV) The teachers of religious law and the Pharisees are the official interpreters of the law of mosses. So practice and obey whatever they tell you, but do not follow their example. For they do not practice what they teach.

They crush people with unbearable religious demands and never lift a finger to ease the burden.

In addition, you should imitate me, just as I imitate Christ. 1 Corinthians 11:1-2 (NIV) I am glad that you always keep me in your thoughts, and that you are following the teaching I passed on to you.

God given wisdom is the only true wisdom, that is why Jesus said man shall not live by bread alone but by every word that comes from the mouth of God.

Many of us talk the talk but we are far from putting the action of the word we speak into practice.

Matthew 7:21-23 (NIV) Not everyone who calls out to me Lord! Lord! Will enter the kingdom of heaven. Only those who actually do the will of my father in heaven will enter.

On judgment day, many will say to me, Lord! We prophesied in your name, cast out demons in your name, and performed many miracles in your name.

But I will reply, I never know you, get away from me, you who break God laws. What we need to understand is, Jesus said the heaven and the earth will pass away but his words will never pass away.

Proverbs 12:15 (NIV) Fools think their own way is right, but the wise listen to others.

Proverbs 12:17 (NIV) An honest witness tells the truth; a false witness tells lies.

Proverbs 13:3 (NIV) Those who control their tongue will have a long life; opening your mouth can ruin everything. The instruction you follow determine the further you create.

To illustrate more, Deuteronomy 30:19-20 (NIV) Today I have given you the choice between life and death, between blessings and curse. Now I call on heaven and earth to witness the choice you make, oh that you would choose life, so that you and your descendant might live!

You can make this choice by loving the Lord your God, obeying him, and committing yourself firmly to him. This is the key to your life.

And if you love and obey the Lord, you will live long in the land the Lord swore to give your ancestors Abraham, Isaac and Jacob.

But the word of the Lord endures forever. And this is the word which by the gospel is preached unto you. The spirit in you and me is greater than the spirit that lives in the world. God created you and me to be Holy. God bless you and keep you safe. His peace passes all understanding.

Prayer To The Lord

I have received the spirit of God: 1 Corinthians 2:12 (NIV) And we have received God's Spirit, not the world's, Spirit, so we can know the wonderful things God has freely given us.

Heavenly father I put my trust in you. Show me any area of my life in which you are not my source and help me to rely on you for my provision. There is no substitute for you in my life. I need you in my life Lord Jesus. Heavenly father God grant me the strength to accept the things I cannot change. Lord give me the courage to change the things I can.

Holy Spirit fill me with the wisdom to know the truth and guide me to live one day at a time in the present moment. In the name of Jesus Christ I pray.

2 Corinthians 10:4-5 (NIV) We use God's mighty weapons, not worldly weapons, to knock down the strongholds of human reasoning and to destroy false arguments. We destroy every proud obstacle that keeps people from God. We capture their rebellious thoughts and teach them to obey Christ.

Laying A Solid Foundation

1 Corinthians 3:11 (NIV) For no one can lay any foundation other than the one we already have Christ Jesus.

We all as God image and likeness were made for a reason and for a purpose. In the world we are living in, we all have to lay a foundation. When I say foundation, I am speaking of something to build on, to stand on, something that is solid.

When God created everything, God saw it was good. When God made man, he made them on a solid foundation; but somewhere along the way, man got broken. When man decided to build their house somewhere else; by listening to someone else who has no knowledge of building on a solid foundation.

Matthew 7:24-27 (NIV) Anyone who listens to my teaching and follows it is wise, like a person who builds a house on solid rock.

Though the rain comes in torrents and the floodwaters rise and winds beat against that house, it will not collapse because it is built on bedrock.

But anyone who hears my teaching and doesn't obey it is foolish, like a person who builds a house on sand.

When the rains and floods come and the winds beat against that house, it will collapse with a mighty crash.

We all had put our time and energy into somethings and we all make choices; in what we say, do and where we go.

No one can lay any foundation other than the one we already have- Jesus Christ.

Prayer To The Lord

Father God thank you for sending your one and only son Jesus Christ as my solid foundation. Thank you Lord for your words of wisdom and guidance, on this life journey to the place you have promise.

Thank you for laying a foundation for others and me to follow. May your love and light be a guide for our eyes, our hearts and feet.

May your children seek you first in all that you commanded them through you beloved son Jesus. All the glory, praise, honor and thanks to you. Your love endures forever.

I pray that your spirit of obedience will continue to fill me and protect me as I summit my life to you. In the name of Jesus I as.

Lord you are my rock and my fortress today I built my life on your foundation. May your seed of love grow deep within me as you feed me with your everlasting living water.

I am bless to build my life on your foundation. Thank you Lord. May you light continues to shine into the heart of everyone. Knowing that you are the way the truth and the life. The eternal one. In the name of Jesus I pray.

Rejection From The World Not From God

Psalm 34:17-20 (NIV) The Lord hears his people when they call for help. He rescues them from all their troubles. The Lord is close to the brokenhearted; he rescues those whose spirits are crushed. The righteous person faces many troubles, but the Lord comes to the rescue each time. For the Lord protects the bones of the righteous; not one of them is broken!

Many are the afflictions of the righteous, but the Lord delivers him out of them all. He keeps all his bones; not one of them is broken.

We are all prone to disappointment and feelings of rejection in many different ways. Example: It could have been in the aftermath of a broken relationship, by our parents, friends, brothers, sisters, work, and by the world; the list could go on and on.

One-person rejection does not mean we are unlovable.

However, we can allow that rejection to determine how we feel and allow that feeling to color our idea of who we are, or we can choose to put that behind us and move forward because of something that is far more lasting.

Psalm 27:10 (NIV) Even if my mother and father abandon me, the Lord will hold me close. The Lord will always take care of you and me, even in the face of rejection.

Honor your mother and your father, for your days shall be long on the earth; they are your parents, if God did not use them, as his vessel, you and I would not be here. It does' not matter who reject you, remember this, Jesus loves you even before you and me were even born.

I think many of us have felt some kind of rejection in our lifetime on this earth. Moreover, many of us have felt like a foreigner in our own home, a stranger in our place of work, or a visitor among your own friends, family and the world.

The Lord loves you and me as his children. 1 John 3:1 (NIV) See how very much our father loves us, for he calls us his children, and that is what we are! But the people who belong to this world don't recognize that we are God's children because they don't know him.

When you are feeling rejected by your feelings, remember you are not alone in this and you had never been alone. However, there is hope when you feel abandoned by others and the world; you can turn to God word for comfort.

Jesus said in John 15:18-19 (NIV) If the world hates you, remember that it hated me first. The world would love you as one of its own if you belong to it, but you are no longer part of the world. I chose you to come out of the world, so it hates you.

Where does the word rejection came from, it came from the world. The word rejection to me is a spirit, a spirit that did not listen to God and were cast out. Moreover a spirit that does not like to see the beauty of God image and likeness in you and me shines.

What blessings await you when people hate you and exclude you and mock you and curse you as evil because you follow the son of man.

The bible tell us in (1 peter 5:8 (NIV) Stay alert! Watch out for your great enemy, the devil. He prowls around live a roaring lion, looking for someone to devour.

When you find yourself tangled in despair, seek the Lord for love, affirmation and acceptance. The Lord wants you and me to experience the fullness of his love; the Lord wants you and me to know that nothing can separate you and me from God love.

I pray that the Lord will fill our spirit with his spirit, the spirit that lives in our Lord Jesus Christ; the same spirit that raise Jesus from the grave. Moreover the spirit that lives in you and me, have the power to rule over everything that lives in the world.

Romans8:38-39 (NIV) And I am convinced that nothing can ever separate us from God's love. Neither death nor life, neither angels nor other demons, neither our fears for today nor our worries about tomorrow – not even the powers of hell can separate us from God's love.

No power in the sky above or in the earth below – indeed, nothing in all creation will ever be able to separate us from the love of God that is revealed in Christ Jesus our Lord.

I pray that you will cast all of your care upon him; for he cares for you. Jesus came into the world unto his own, and his own received him not.

Therefore, if you are a child of God, you may suffer disappointment and rejection in this life, but you need to remember that as a child of the king, this rejection is a momentary bump in the road.

You have a choice to either allow that bump to derail you and walk wounded, or you can choose to claim the heritage of a child of God and move forward in grace.

Forgiveness of others and of self is a gift that you can give because it is the gift given to you and me by the Lord Jesus Christ.

Matthew 11:28-30 (NIV) Than Jesus said, come to me, all of you who are weary and carry heavy burdens, and I will give you rest. Take my yoke upon you. Let me teach you, because I am humble and gentle at heart, and you will find rest for your souls. For my yoke is easy to bear, and the burden I give is light.

Pray To The Lord

Father God of our Lord Jesus; thank you for your love, your grace and your mercy. Thank you Lord for letting me know that I can come to you at all time. Lord I know you care for others and me with the love we cannot fine anywhere; but only in you.

Lord Jesus thank you for filling my heart with the depth of your love and the peace of understanding. Thank you Lord for the light that overwhelm the darkness. Thank you Lord for your healing hands, the love and care in them.

Lord Jesus I am yours because I was created in your image and your likeness. Lord continue to bless me so I can be a blessing; may your love continue to flow in me like a never-ending river.

Lord I command the spirit of rejection, when people rejected me, my friends rejected me, my parents rejected me, my family rejected me and the world rejected me, to come out of me now in the name of Jesus.

I command the spirit of rejection and self-rejection to come all the way out of me and leave me now never to return in the name of Jesus.

I receive acceptance from you Lord, you are my father and I know you love me. I command out of me every spirit that attacks my physical body and my life.

I command them to leave and never come back. In the name of Jesus, I break the power of all spirits that is causing any problems in my life.

Than you Lord, I forgive everyone that offended me and I ask you please to bless him and her. In the name of Jesus, I submit, I humble myself and release everything to you. Amen.

What Dominates Our Mind
Is What We Obey.

John 1: 2-15 (KJV) Love not the world, neither the things that are in the world. If any man loves the world, the love of the father is not in him.

What dominates our mind?

Moreover, many things can dominate our mind, our body, our heart, our spirit and our soul. Example) our thoughts have a big part to play in our everyday lives. In what and whom we obey; many of us as Christians and non-Christians struggle with these issue, especially in our technological world. However, with cell phones, the television and many objects that is taking over the world and our mind.

Likewise, the world we are living in today is not how it use to be; it seems like it has become a place to dominate and project the things in it to control our lives.

We are children of God; we are made in his image and his likeness. Furthermore, we were made to be like him, think like him and do the things he made you and me do.

Proverbs 4:23 (NIV) Guard your heart above all else, for it determines the course of your life. The heart includes the mind and all that proceeds from it.

Therefore, whatever you spend your time and whom you give your time to, and spent it with, will determine your outcome. Can we move forward without looking back?

There is a saying sometime you have to go into the past so you can move forward. The way out is to go through the things that been holing us back; to exit we have to enter.

All the problems we face and go through, it started at the root. The things that we are claiming are the things that will dominate our mind.

Who and what are we fighting; are we fighting to be or to become? Nothing is yours, our battle in the world is our flesh, the world and the devil.

Jesus said he is the way the truth and the life. Jesus is the only way back to our heavenly father; the father of all creation, things seen and unseen. Jesus is the foundation of our lives. In the beginning was the word and the word were with God and God is the word.

1 Corinthians 3:11 (KJV) For other foundation can no ma lay that that is laid, which is Jesus Christ.

We are always going to be tempted, by the temper of this world, the adversary, that old serpent; moreover, temptation is necessary in the world we are living in today.

Question- what do we do when we feel that we are being temped. Remember the power of life and death is in our tongue. The tongue has the power to speak blessing, defeat and curse. Those who love to speak will reap the benefit from it.

It is important to understand that when a thought enters our mind, we should examine it based upon God's word and determine if we should continue down that path or reject the thought and replace it with another thought.

Moreover, if we have already allowed a habit to form in our thought lives, it becomes more difficult to change the path of our thoughts.

Example- when we sow a seed we expect it to grow into something (a tree) and when it start to grow; do we take care of it, or do we let it take care of itself.

We need to prune our thoughts. Just like how a gardener is going to prune the branches of a tree.

Likewise, every word and thought is a seed. Do you let someone, or anyone to enter in your house without knocking? On the other hand, do you let them enter into your home and then ask them questions after.

We were all seeds before we became who we are today. Moreover, when we help grow up a child mind, him or her, when their mind is young, it can be hard to get the thought out of their mind.

It depends on how you raise him or her, and what you put into them. The bible said train up a child when they are young with the word of God so when they get older it will not depart from them.

Here are some biblical suggestion for taking control of our thoughts. Live in dependence upon the Holy Spirit, through seeking his strength through prayer.

Matthew 26:41 (NIV) Keep watch and pray, so that you will not give into temptation. For the spirit is willing, but the body is weak.

If we rely upon our own strength, we will fail. Proverbs 28:26 (NIV) Those who trust their own insight are foolish, but anyone who walks in wisdom is safe.

We are not to feed our minds with things that will promote negative thoughts and idea that will dominate our minds. We need to feed our minds with the word and love of God.

Furthermore, we are to guard our hearts and mind what we allow into them and what we allow them to dwell on.

Indeed, we are to pursue hard after God, with godly mindset. When tempted to hate someone are anything else, we replace those thoughts with godly actions and love:

If you are an apple tree, apple is what you will produce. If you are a child of God his image and likeness is what you will reflect.

Example – when someone (a person) or something come against you in a hateful way, what will you do, will you change who you are to be like them:

No, we do good to them, speak well of them, and pray for them; if we choose to treat them the way they treat you. You are not portraying who you say you are; a true apple cannot change to be something different than what it is. Get out of your head and think, get into your heart. Think less, feel more.

If we are not seeking and replacing the thoughts that are dominating our mind with godly ones; it will leave an empty field for Satan to come along and sow his weeds.

If you look carefully, you will see life is like a mirror, it reflects your face. It can be friendly and all of life will reflect friendliness to you.

God will bless those who seek to honor him with what matters most to him; who we are inside and not just what we appear to be to others on the outside.

Be in God's words so that when a thought that can dominate our mind, we can examine it based upon God word and determine if we should continue down that path or reject the thought and replace it with another thought.

Ephesians 4:23-24 (NIV) Instead, let the spirit renew your thoughts and attitudes. Put on your new nature, created to be like God truly righteous and holy.

Prayer To The Lord

Lord Jesus thank you for loving me as I am. Lord Jesus I come to you just as I am. Lord draw me close to your side, renew my mind as I see you unfold in power, light and love.

Lord Jesus hold me close in the power of your love. Lord Jesus you are my desire and my friend. Lord, nothing else could take your place in my heart and my life.

Lord Jesus I am alive and well because your spirit lives in me. Lord Jesus I give you all my discouragement, all my stress, all my plans, all my hurts, all my love and all my trust.

Lord Jesus I ask you to empty me of all of me and fill me with all of you. Lord Jesus I want to feel your love deep within my spirit, heart and soul.

Lord Jesus continue to bless my eyes to seek you and to fine you in everything I do, with every breath and heartbeat.

Thank you Lord for restoring my broken heart and bringing me back to who I am in you. Lord Jesus continue to fill my lungs to sing and praise you for all the earth to hear.

Lord Jesus let the words that comes from my mouth, let it be your words that you put into my heart. This I pray and ask in the name of our Lord and savior Jesus Christ. I receive Amen.

It Is An Inside Job

In Matthew, Jesus in the wilderness responded to each of Satan's temptation with scripture that applied to the direction he knew his mind should take instead of going down the path of the sinful thought.

Jesus was tempted by Satan to meet his physical need (example) turn stone into bread, Jesus has recited the passage about the importance of relying upon God.

When Jesus was tempted to serve Satan in order to obtain the glory of the world, Jesus brought up the passage that says we are to serve and worship God alone and speak of the glory that belongs to him and those who are his.

Furthermore, when Jesus was tempted to test God (to see if God was really there and would keep his promises), Jesus responded with a passages that stress the importance of believing God without having to see him demonstrate.

We need to put on the Lord Jesus Christ and make no provision for the flesh, to fulfill its lust.

1 John 2:16 (NIV) For the world offers only a craving for physical pleasure, a craving for everything we see, and pride in our achievements and possessions. These are not from the father, but

are from along with everything that people crave. But anyone who does what pleases God will live forever.

We are to be more aware and avoid watching certain television shows, videos, websites, internet entertainment music, video game and the conversations and situations that will sets us up for a fall.

That is why we should also avoid spending time with those who would encourage us down these wrong paths.

The internet and all forms of social media are some of the devil's tools, as the bible says the devil is the prince of the power of the air. The devil will use the means of the things in the world and the media to try to take control over our lives. Through these gateways the devil will try everything he can to distract us.

Moreover, many of the movies, the music and the cartoons we are letting our children watch are filled with occult activity; some of the most innocent (so called) movies and music are filled with garbage that will dull our minds and vision.

The gateways of our soul are the eyes, the ear and the mouth. These are our spiritual gates.

(Mouth gate)-The words we speak can bring a blessing or it can bring a curse; it can also build us up or tear us down.

Therefore we should guard our mouths from speaking things that are harmful not only towards others, but toward ourselves. It is important to think before you speak, because many who listen to you may be subjected to what is in your heart.

There is a saying if you have nothing nice to say, do not say anything at all. Even if it is about yourself. The things that proceed out of the mouth come from the heart, and those things defile a person.

(Ear gate)-The ear can hear the things that can lead us on the right path or the wrong one; that is why we need to learn and know the voice of God. What we hear and listen too strongly affect our minds whether consciously or subconsciously.

There are all sorts of things we hear that shape our thoughts, our decision and our actions. Even when taking advice and listening to people, it is normal for us to listen to people tell us what we want to hear to help us justify what we know in our hearts is not right. So be careful who and what you listening too.

Eye gate Luke 11: 34 (NIV) Your eye is a lamp that provides light for your body. When your eye is good, your whole body is filled with light. But when it is bad, your body is filled with darkness.

Have you ever heard of the phrase, "eyes are the windows to the soul? According to the Bible, that is very true.

It is very important to evaluate what you watch. Things that we see, if not careful, it can manifest in our hearts and minds and eventually turn into action.

Provers 4:23 (NIV) Guard your heart above all else, for it determines the course of your life.

Give thanks to the Lord, for he is good! His faithful love endures forever.

2 Corinthians 7:1 (NIV) Because we have these promise, dear friends, let us cleanse ourselves from everything that can defile our body or spirit. Moreover, let us work toward complete holiness because we fear God.

2 Corinthians 6: 10 (NIV) Our heart ache, but we always have joy. We are poor, but we give spiritual riches to others. We own nothing, and yet we have everything.

In everything seek God first; above all, God will bless those who seek to honor him, what matters most to him: who we are inside and not just what we appear to be to others on the outside.

Our identity is in God through our Lord Jesus Christ, love, joy, peace, and the light of his image and his likeness.

The devil wants to steal our identity by the thoughts he try to put into our mind. The devil comes to kill, steal and destroy. The devil plans is to try to steal our identity from God our father.

The devil plans is to try to destroy what God had created you and me to be. Jesus said that he came that we may have life and have it more abundantly.

2 Corinthians 3:4-6 (NIV) We are confident of all this because of our great trust in God through Christ. It is not that we think we are qualified to do anything on our own. Our qualification comes from God.

He has enabled us to be ministers of his new covenant. This is a covenant not of written laws, but of the spirit. The old written covenant ends in death; but the spirit gives life.

Be open to advice and instruction; Proverbs 19:20 (NIV) Get all the advice and instruction you can, so you will be wise the rest of your life.

Most people have it back to front, believing that they feel or think a certain way because of their circumstances, not knowing the truth that it is their thought power of words that is creating those very circumstances, whether wanted or unwanted.

Our thoughts and words are alive. Proverbs 18:21 (NIV) The tongue can bring death or life; those who love to talk will reap the consequences.

Deuteronomy 30:19 (NIV) Today I have given you the choice between life and death, between blessings and curse. Now I call on heaven and earth to witness the choice you make. Oh, that you would choose life, so that your descendants might live!

Do you know the voice of God for your life? On the other hand, have you been listening to the voice of the devil?

A Prayer To Be Restored

Father God in the name of Jesus. I want to thank you for creating me in your image and your likeness.

I pray for your Holy Spirit Lord to fill and lead me to the places you want me to go. Lord Jesus I know you will strengthen me when it seem like my strength is failing.

Lord Jesus shine your light in my eyes so I can see everything the way you see them. Lord reminded me of who you created me to be on the inside.

Lord thank you for your wisdom and your understanding to know the things and the people of the world have no power to hurt me, with their word, or to change me to be who I am not.

Lord Jesus thank you for your shield, your love and your spirit that reigns in me forever and ever, all the days of my life.

Lord Jesus I have found your peace that made me whole. Father God I find rest for my soul in the depths of your love for me.

Lord Jesus your spirit of trust lives in me, with a sealed and a promise that cannot be broken. Lord God almighty you are worthy to be praise. All the glory and praise is yours.

Lord Jesus you know what is in my heart, you created it. Lord fill my spirit to stay faithful no matter what I may face.

Lord Jesus strengthen my mind, my heart and my spirit, from the worries and the things in the world.

Lord fill my spirit to rejoice in all the things I may face and hear from the people of the world, Who do not know you. In Jesus name, I pray.

Lord Jesus let your glory shine in me, fill my ear with your sweet, sweet sound of peace for my soul.

Lord empty me from everything that is not from you, fill me with more of you. In Jesus mighty name, I pray. All the glory, the honor, the power and the praises is your now and forever. Amen.

Contentment

Hebrews 13:5 (NIV) Don't love money; be satisfied with what you have. For God said, I will never fail you. I will never abandon you."

In today world, it is rare that we find anyone contented with his or her condition in life. The state of us being mentally, emotionally, financially or physically satisfied with things as they are. Moreover, with the things, we have and with the people that is in our life.

The bible has a great deal to say about contentment – being satisfied with what we have, who we are, and where we are going.

Jesus said that he is the way the truth and the life; when it seems like there is no way Jesus will make away for you and for me.

The father will always give us what our heart desire, all we have to do is believe, ask and continue to put our trust, hope, faith and love in him.

In Matthew 6:25 (NIV) Jesus said, that is why I tell you not to worry about everyday life – whether you have enough food and drink, or enough clothes to wear. Isn't life more than food and your body more than clothing?

Jesus said do not worry about these things, Jesus is also telling us to be content with what we have. Moreover, Jesus has given us a direct command not to worry about the things in the world.

If you look closely, you will see that many of us are still living like the pagans, running after all these things in the world. When our heavenly father knows that, we need them.

Matthew 6:33-34 (NIV) Seek the kingdom of God above all else, and live righteously, and he will give to you everything you need. So do not worry about tomorrow, for tomorrow will bring its own worries. Today's trouble is enough for today.

Moreover, many of us will say that we trust God to provide for our everyday needs. Nevertheless, when we are face with challenging times, many of us faith and trust in God start to disappear.

We worry about everything that is in the world; the things that does not have any power over us. The things of the world that we are worry about, is the same things that is dominating the thoughts of unbelievers.

We have a father who loves you and me more than we can ever imagine. That is why Jesus said do not worry about what to eat, what to drink and what to wear. If God can care and clothed the lilies of the field today;

Matthew 7:6- 30 (NIV) And if God cares so wonderfully for wildflowers that are here today and thrown into fire tomorrow, he will certainly care for you. Why do you have so little faith?

To worry means we do not trust God. The key to overcome discontentment and lack of faith is to find out who God really is and how he has been faithful to supply the need of his people in the past. The God of our Lord Jesus Christ is the same yesterday, today and forever.

The Studying of our heavenly father and the promises he had made for you and I; it will help us grow our confidence and trust in him for the future.

Jeremiah 29:11 (NIV) For I know the plans I have for you," says the Lord. They are plans for good and not for disaster, to give you a future and a hope.

We need to humble ourselves before God, under his mighty hands he will lift us up in due time. Let us cast all of our worries and anxiety on him because he cares for you and me.

Furthermore, let us wait on the Lord so he can renew our mind, strengthen our heart and give us wings to fly like eagles, feet to run and not to get weary.

Matthew 6:21 (NIV) Wherever your treasure is, there the desires of your heart will also be.

The apostle Paul was a man who suffered and when without the comfort of life more than most people could ever imagine.

Philippians 4:12-13 (NIV) I know how to live on almost nothing or with everything. I have learned the secret of living in every situation, whether it is with a full stomach or empty, with plenty or little. For I can do everything through Christ, who gives me strength.

The Lord is my helper, he is my provider he always goes before me; I will not fear. What can man do to me?

Yet many people continue to seek after more of the things of this world, never contented with their lot in life.

Beware of greed life is more than stuff. If we are not content with what we have, we envy others or keep chasing after empty things.

Moreover, many of us who own a car or have a house; whenever we see someone who has a brand name new car or a bigger house than what they have.

The lust of the flesh and the greed of their heart start to take them over; likewise many people think that the more money, and the value of the things that they have in the world, that It will make their lives worth more.

Whoever loves money never has enough; whoever loves wealth is never satisfied with his income.

Proverbs 11:4 (NIV) Riches will not help on the Day of Judgment, but right living can save you from death. The richness of your spirit.

Proverbs 11:28 (NIV) Trust in your money and down you go! Nevertheless, the godly flourish like leaves in spring.

Those who desire to be rich fall into temptation. Greedy people are never satisfied with what they have. When asking for something and they do not receive it;

It can be because their motives are wrong. Many of us will ask only for the things so we can spend it on our own selfish passion.

We work so hard to gain the things in the world. This attitude robs us of our joy and we cannot be happy or enjoy the blessing we have. We should be working hard for the things that will feed our spirit.

Proverbs 15:13 (NIV) A glad heart makes a face; a broken heart crushes the spirit.

Learn to be content, trust God, and be at peace. The fear of the Lord leads to life, so that one may sleep satisfied, untouched by evil.

The Lord direct the steps of the godly, he will never let them fall; the Lord holds them in his hands.

Psalm 37:3-5 (NIV) Trust in the Lord and do good. Then you will live safely in the land and prosper. Take delight in the Lord, and he will give you your heart's desires. Commit everything you do to the Lord. Trust him, and he will help you.

That is why we should try believing more in what the Lord had done for you and me; than we having to see before we can believe. Blessed is he who has not seen and still believes and blessed is he who has seen and still believes what the Lord had said and done.

Each man must remain in that condition in which he was called. Do not take money from anyone by force, or accuse anyone falsely, and be content with your wages.

Roman 6:23 (NIV) For the wages of sin is death, but the free gift of God is eternal life through Christ Jesus our Lord.

A Prayer To Be Content

Every word of God proves true. He is a shield to all who come to him for protection.

Thank you father God of our Lord Jesus Christ for your love, your grace and the breath in our lungs.

Dear Lord Jesus, please help us to never be consumed with chasing after material things because it shows a lack of trust in you.

Lord Jesus help us always to remember that life is more than stuff. Lord continue to bless and guide us so we may continually be a blessing to others and to experience true joy, true peace and true contentment.

Lord Jesus let your love be found in loving you, loving me, loving others and being grateful in enjoying all the wonderful gifts yon have blessed us with.

Lord Jesus keep deception and lies far from me give me neither poverty nor riches; feed me with the food that is my portion. In Jesus name I pray Amen.

How Honest Are You

Psalms 51:6 (NIV) But you desires honesty from the womb, teaching me wisdom even there.

Honesty is the virtue of truthfulness in relating to all the issues of life. Honesty is really a heart matter. It is a fundamental truth of the gospel of our Lord Jesus Christ.

God knows the thoughts and intention of the heart. He regards truth as a most important principle because he is God of truth.

If you know the truth and speak the truth, it will set you free. What is the truth many will ask; the word from God our heavenly father of our Lord Jesus Christ.

The truth is the words spoken by our Lord Jesus Christ, and it was put into action by the love he shared. A tree produce what it is.

God will surely bless those who are completely honest in heart. God knows our heart because he created it. When God look at a person, he looks at his and her heart.

Do you tell the truth when you might be found out? On the other hand, do you tell less of the truth than be honest?

Many of us will knowingly leave someone with the false impression of something that is not true. Do you tell God how it really is when you pray?

Are you one of the people that pretend to be something you are not?

There is an impressive story in the new testament of the Bible of a man, Ananias and his wife Sapphira.

In acts 5:1-4 (NIV) But there was a certain man named Ananias who, with his wife, Sapphira, sold some property.

He brought part of the money to the apostles, claiming it was the full amount. With his wife's consent, he kept the rest.

Then peter said, Ananias, why have you let Satan fill your heart? You lied to the Holy Spirit, and you kept some of the money for yourself.

The property was your to sell or not to sell, as you wished. And after selling it, the money was also your to give away. How could you do a thing like this? You were not lying to us but to God.

We may give a false impression even though the words that are spoken are not a lie. We tend to forget our accountability before God. He knows our hearts and expects complete honesty.

Many of the times, we think we are lying to others and God but we are lying to ourselves.

A hypocrite pretends to be someone he and she are not. He and she may claim to be truthful, but are not careful when it is his and her advantage to stretch the truth.

Many of us will talk of the needs of the unfortunate people, but we are not that generous to give our time and money when disasters strikes. Someone may pretend to be genuinely concerned about his and her neighbors, and yet find it easy to gossip about them.

One may pose as an honest person, but still be ready to take someone else's money as long as he or she is not caught.

Furthermore, he or she may even try to convince himself or herself that they are living according to a higher standards of conduct than others do; while they themselves are being deceitful.

Moreover, pride and selfishness was the fall of the human races. So do not think you are better or smarter than anyone else is.

The hypocrisy of man has always grieved God heart. Jesus said, people draw night unto me with their mouth, and honor me with their lips; but their heart is far from me.

The heart and lips of a person together is a challenge. Honesty from the core of our being is the key to find grace and favor with the Lord.

A true person from God is an example of honesty. We were made in God image and likeness. Likewise, many of us will prosper spiritually when we are in a direct relationship in being honest before God.

The importance of honesty in relation to our fellowman also deserves careful attention; both in word and out word dealings. In order to do this, we must be willing to make any sacrifice for the sake of the truth.

Honesty is a test of character. God knows our hearts, and there is nothing hidden from him. However, we sometimes do not relate to God as he knows us and as we really fell inside. We may not portray our honest or true self to the public.

Likewise, our motives and attitudes need to be submitted to the honesty test; as we open our hearts and lives to God, all these issues can be resolved. The true happiness of a person is one who is honest with God and admits who he really is.

Are you honest? God requires it, the world expects it, and you will benefit from it. It is the only life that pays.

Furthermore, in all things be willing to live honesty with a clear conscience and in everything, we do and say; let it be through Christ Jesus who gives us strength.

Romans 12:17-18 (NIV) Never pay back evil with more evil. Do things in such a way that everyone can see you are honorable. Do all that you can to live in peace with everyone.

Proverbs 17:20 (NIV) The crooked heart will not prosper; the lying tongue tumbles into trouble.

Proverbs 17:5 (NIV) A false witness will not go unpunished, nor will a liar escape.

The Lord said you must be careful to keep all my decrees and regulations by putting them into practice. Do not let anyone mislead you.

Deuteronomy 32:4 (KJV) He is a rock, his work is perfect: for all his ways are judgment: a God of truth and without iniquity, just and right is he.

A Prayer To The Lord

Heavenly father of our Lord Jesus Christ. I humbly come to you in spirit asking you to cleanse me from within out, cleanse my heart, my spirit man and make in me a new heart. Lord, I surrender all my cares and ways to you. Lord, I ask your forgiveness, love and mercy.

Lord Jesus fill my thoughts and my heart with your spirit of truth. Lord let the word that comes from my heart let it be your word.

Lord Jesus created in me an honest heart and a renewed spirit. Lord strengthen me to speak the true so it can set me free. May the light of Jesus continue to shine the way for me to the way to you father God.

Lord Jesus I come to you with a spirit to be honest in every areas of my heart. Lord, you have commanded the virtue of honesty; it is the power against all deceptions.

Lord Jesus direct your spirit of honesty upon me. Guide my daily thoughts, words and action, to join those living by the spirit of truth.

Lord Jesus I choose to be still before you, speak to my heart and fill me with peace as I put my trust and faith in you. This I pray, declare and receive in the name of Jesus. Amen.

The Key For Love

When the heart cries, no one knows. Only God, he will be our shoulder to cry on.

All are welcome. When the heart smiles with joy. Feeling the key of one love entering into our lock of chains.

Now you know where that smile came from, God. The I am, the Christ, the one and only.

The mile you took in finding that smile. Show that you are a fighter not a victim.

The key of love is in the air, filling each heart with faith. Looking up into the sky.

Seeing the lights of the stars shining into the eye of our soul; saying well come back.

The sheep of the pastures. Found my way, now I am here to stay. Never be afraid to say who you are in the key of love. The I am.

Prayer To The Lord

Father God of our Lord Jesus Christ. I want to say thank you for creating me with such a beauty. Thank you Lord for all that, you created me in your image and your likeness. I humbly come to you seeking rest for my heart, mind, spirit and soul with thanksgiving.

Lord Jesus I am here to declare and to praise you. I am bless in the name of Jesus. I am healthy in the name of Jesus. I am rich in the name of Jesus. I am beautiful from the inside out in the name of Jesus.

Thank you Lord for the breath I take and the strength to say thank you. Lord Jesus continue to fill my heart with the desire to worship and honor you in spirit and in truth.

I am healed in the name of Jesus. I am covered with the precious blood of Jesus. I am full of the joy of the Lord strength in the name of Jesus.

Thank you Lord Jesus for your touch of peace in my heart and my spirit. I am safe in the name of Jesus. I am found in the name of Jesus Christ for all eternity.

I am shield with the promise of our Lord Jesus Christ. I am an image and likeness of God in the name of Jesus.

I am free in the name of Jesus. I am alive in the name of Jesus. I am a child of God in the name of Jesus. I am perfect in the eyes and name of our Lord Jesus.

Lord Jesus you are perfect in all of your ways. All the glory, the honor, the praise and the power is your Lord.

I have victory the name of Jesus. I am delivered in the name of Jesus. I am wise in the name of Jesus. I am humble in the name of Jesus. I am creative in the name of Jesus.

No weapon form against me shall prosper in the name of Jesus; every tongue that rise against me shall not prosper in the name of Jesus.

The light of Jesus is upon me, before me, behind me and around me. I walk in divined health in the name of Jesus.

I am financially bless in the name of Jesus. My hand are bless in the name of Jesus. I am bless in my going out and in my coming in, in the name of Jesus.

The hedge of protection of Jesus is over me.

Lord Jesus there is none like you; Lord, you are awesome and powerful in all your way.

Lord Jesus your name is above all names, thank you in all that you do, done and still doing for others and me.

All the glory, the honor and the praises in your now and forever within my heart you created. In the name of our Lord Jesus Christ, I declare and receive. Amen

Honor My Mother And Father

Colossians 3:20 (KJV) Children, obey your parents, in all things; for this is well pleasing unto the Lord.

Honoring your father and mother is being respectful in words, action, and having an inward attitude of esteem for their position.

Honoring is giving respect; we are living in a world where you can see that honoring and respecting fathers and mothers are getting out of control.

However, many may disagree with their parent's decisions, but they should still respect their parent's decisions.

Likewise, children of all ages should honor and respect their parents, regardless of whether or not their parents deserve honor.

Moreover, God exhorts us to honor father and mother. God values honoring parents enough to include it in the Ten Commandments.

Exodus 20:12 (KJV) Honor thy father and thy mother: that thy days may be long upon the land which the Lord thy God giveth thee.

Honor your father and mother, which is the first commandment with a promise; and it is a scripture that promises long life as a reward. Those who honor their parents are bless.

Solomon, the wisest man had urged children to respect their parents.

Proverbs 1:8 (KJV) My son hear the instruction of thy father, and forsake not the law of thy mother.

A wise son hearth his father's instruction: but a scorner hearth not rebuke.

Proverbs 30:17 (KJV) The eye that mocks a father and despises a mother's instructions will be plucked out by ravens of the valley and eaten by vultures.

We cannot outgrow God's command to honor our parents, even Jesus, God the son, submitted himself to both his earthy parents.

Honoring our parents is one of the greatest blessings you and I can receive and have. We may have to make decisions that our parents disagree with.

There are many reasons why I said that; (Example) in a society where knowledge is prized more than wisdom for many of us. Today children's are learning things that parents never hear of.

Moreover, each new generation quickly surpasses the preceding generation in the knowledge it possesses; many of us will blame or do not speak to our parents for many different reason. Whatever the reason may have been, it is still your parents, you need to forgive and do your best for them.

We are living in a time where things and people are being process in to an operation that affects many of us mentally.

I watch a scene where a young woman and her mother were in a courtroom. The young woman was blaming her mother because of the way she grew up. There is something you should try to understand, back them, in the (1960-1980) was much different from the time we are now living in today.

Many of us don't even have any idea what our parents had to go through to take care of you and I. let us not try to blame our parents; instead lets be more thankful and try to understand and show them our love and respect them.

As I said earlier, in the time, places were, and how our parents live their lives, were much different from how we are living our lives today.

Many parents had to do what they had to do to take care of you and me. What we have now was not accessible to our parents back then. The education, the transportation and the resources.

Prayer For Honoring Our Parents Father And Mother

Heavenly father of our Lord Jesus Christ; you are the only perfect parent. Thank you for the breath of life, and for giving me my earthy parents who bring me fort with your love, image and likeness.

Father I thank you for my dearest parents who have loved me and cared for me. Lord Jesus I pray and ask you to be with them and surround them with your presence, keep them safe and fill them with your love.

Lord Jesus open their hearts to trust your constant care. Help me Lord to show my parents how much I appreciate and love them. Lord forgive me for all the times I have made them sad.

Lord Jesus continue to bless my parents with good health, love, peace and happiness. Lord, I place them in your hands; watch over them with tender love and care. Lord I pray that you keep them close to one another in this life and in the next.

Lord, I pray that the responsibility that they have, you will guide and give them the strength to go through it; and to seek you first in all that they do.

May your love give them comfort, peace and direction in what they have to do. Lord may our parents be fill with your Holy Spirit and your every lasting love. In the name of Jesus, I pray. Amen.

Crossroad

Jeremiah 6:16 (NIV) This what the Lord says. Stop at the crossroad and look around. Ask for the old, godly way, and walk in it. Travel its path, and you will find rest for your souls. But you reply, no, that's not the road we want.

A journey we are all on to seek the truth, not from man, nor woman and not from new age; however, from the truth itself. A cross road where there is darkness and light, old and new. Where do I go, that is a question of a lifetime.

A Desire for something that does not last for long in a world filled with the desires for pleasure. Bellies are full but they are still hungry. Many souls are crying out for satisfaction. The image of love is what I can see. A crossroad with no signs.

At a point when a choice must be made. I need to figure out which direction my life should take. Life creates many opportunity for us to choose between, different options; and when we see someone embracing the moment.

There is a way that seems right unto man, but the end thereof is the ways of death. Likewise, north or south, east or west which course will you take-God will or your own way? The choice is up to you.

Trust in the Lord with all thine heart, and lean not unto thine own understanding in all thy ways acknowledge him, and he shall direct thy paths.

A certain path or course of action seems right, that is no guarantee it is right; each must ask ourselves one important question in true obedience.

The old paths are the only paths; to exit I had to enter the old, not to change it but to grow and learn with it.

The choice of roads ahead, but also importantly, looking back at the way by which I have come. Your word is a lamp to my feet and a light to my path. Lord Jesus you are the only way to the heavenly father.

Prayer For Direction

Heavenly father in the name of Jesus Christ I humble and submit my life to you. Thank you for the breath of life and your love.

Lord Jesus teach me the way in which I should walk; for to you I lift up my soul. Lord I pray for your spirit of wisdom and discernment. Lord Jesus guide me in your truth and teach me, for you are the God of my salvation.

You are my rock and my fortress Lord, in all my ways father God give me direction. Lord I ask for the spirit to acknowledge God and for him to make my paths straight. Thank you father God in the name of Jesus Christ, Amen.

Living To Die To Self

Life is like a gust of wind it comes and goes at any time; life is like a season, but it has a meaning, even those many of us do not fully understand the reason. Life is like a seed, for a seed to give life it has to put into the ground and die for it to give life.

Life is a gift of love from God, with his breath deep within our soul. First you and I have to find out who created life, and what life is all about.

The word gave life with the breath he took to create you and me. What a beauty and a blessing to be created in the image and likeness of God.

The word is Jesus Christ. In the beginning was the word, and the word was with God, and the word was God.

We are all living to die in the flesh, so we can fully live in the spirit.

John 12:24 (KJV) Verily, verily, I say unto you, except a corn of wheat fall into the ground and die, it abided alone: but if it die, it bringeth forth much fruit.

Matthew 16:25 (KJV) For whoever will save his life shall lose it; and whoever will lose his life for my sake shall find it.

Rejoice In The Storm And Trials

Romans 12:12 (KJV) Rejoicing in hope; patient in tribulation; continuing instant in prayer.

Consider it pure joy, my brothers and sister, whenever you face trials of many kind. Rejoice in the Lord sing praises and give thanks in everything.

You may not understand what I am saying now, but you will find out when you try what I am saying to you. The Lord knows what we are going through and he knows what we may face and encounter in this world.

The storm may come in the evening, but the joy comes in the morning. The joy of the Lord is our strength.

When difficult times come into our lives and we find ourselves unable to comprehend/ to understand; rejoice in the Lord be glad, sing, dance and call out to Jesus giving thank in everything.

We may find ourselves questioning God's goodness/ God wisdom is allowing these things to happen. Therefore, we may see that there is victory in every storm; God want you and me to know that whatever we may encounter any kind of trail, he is always here for us.

We are never alone and there is nothing in the world that can separate you and me from the love God have for us.

We go through trials in life for us to grow stronger and for us to depend on God and not on our own understanding and strength.

We may even be bitter and angry with God for allowing this to happen to us and wonder if he really cares. Yes, I believe God cares for you and for me; for God so love the world that he gave his one and only son. God does not allow anything to happen to us, it is the choices we make when we go through the trials in our lives.

Likewise when you and me was small growing up to become teenager our parents will discipline us, when we did something wrong; that does not mean that our parents do not care or love us. Most of our parents will discipline their children and some will not. However, some will learn the easy way and some will have to learn the hard way.

But Gods word confidently reminds us that God does understand. However, things do not just happen without no meaning, reason or no purpose.

God is in control even in our most difficult times and in our circumstances. God wants us to trust him in the trials of life. As we put out trust in God in our trials. You will get to see that God can use the difficult trial to mild us; to mature us so that we will be more like Jesus Christ our savior.

What do you do when you are going through a trail in your life? The first question many of us will or may ask is why me, what have I done.

Let us change our why in to what it is Lord you want me to see and do in my trials. Lord Jesus I am asking you now for direction and guidance.

We go through trails in our lives to help us grow spiritually and to help us mature and become more like Christ.

I read a story about a man, who went out at sea with his boat on a trip. Somewhere along his trip, he ran into some trouble. His boat was shipwreck and his boat began to sink. The man was in middle of the ocean.

When he had to make the choice to go down with his boat or swim to safety for his life. The man decided to jump over board into the water; he began to swim for safety when he saw something like a piece of island.

However, it was a little piece of island he had seen. The man continued to swim to the island he had seen, eventually he made it to safety;

After arriving safely, the man took a rest after the long swim to safety. The man looks around and called out to see if there was anyone else on the piece of island.

It seems like the man was the only person on the island. The man began to build a shack (house) where he can rest his head. The next day the man tried to get of the piece of island.

The man began to pray to God asking him for his help to be rescued off the island; after the man had finish praying to God, he found pieces of wood and began putting them together to make a life raft.

Nevertheless, the man was not successful in all that he has tried using to make, to get of the island. The man prayed to God again and after praying, he went for a walk, throughout the island to see what he can find to make something else to help him get of the island.

The man decided to go back to the little house he had built. The man thought that he had enough things to make another raft; on his way, back to the little house the man saw that there was smoke in the air. The man began to run toward the direction where he saw the smoke coming from; on his way there, he saw it was his little house on fire.

The man fell to his knee and called out to God with a cry and he weep saying, what next. A little while after the man, look up and saw a little boat coming toward the shore where he is.

A man in a little boat came to the island and the man on the island was happy to see him. The man on the island ask the man that came in the little boat how do you know I was on the island, the man reply I saw the smoke and the fire from afar. I had this feeling. Therefore, I decided to check it out.

Thanks be to God. When we find ourselves unable to see the good and the purpose in trials, we are to pray, keep on asking God for wisdom and continue to have faith in him; remember with God all things are possible, all you have to do is believe.

In addition, our God who loves to give will respond so that we can see the good and the purpose in trials. God promises to make something good out of the storms that bring devastation to your life.

Psalms 91:1 (KJV) He that dwelled in the secret place of the most high shall abide under the shadow of the almighty.

In everything, give thanks even in our trails. Rejoice evermore, pray without ceasing. The Lord tells us that we are to have an attitude of joy, thanksgiving and prayer at all times no matter what the conditions or circumstances are, that surround us.

Our prayers should be in an attitude of praise even in the midst of our trails we should lift our voices and praise the Lord like this.

Father God, I praise you and love you, and no matter what the devil is doing to me I know that you shall bring me through victoriously.

Lord Jesus show me what I need to do; show me the door that I have opened to the enemy. I humble and submit myself to you Lord Jesus, I resist the enemy in the name of Jesus Christ, and I command him to leave with all his oppression and attacks.

Jesus you are the Lord of my life, and I submit to you and will never deny you, no matter what may happen. Praise and glory to God of our Lord Jesus Christ. Amen.

Prayer When Going Through Trials

Father God of our Lord Jesus Christ I humbly come to you knowing that you are the bread of life; and I cannot do this on my own understanding. Lord Jesus I submit all of me and everything to you.

Lord Jesus I pray for your guidance; Lord in every need let me come to you with a humble heart and a trusting spirit in Jesus name I pray.

Thank you Lord for creating me in your image and your likeness. Thank you for the breath of life and your unfailing love.

Lord Jesus in all my doubts, temptation, loneliness, weariness, trails, failure, disappointment, trouble, and sorrow. Help me Jesus to be an overcomer in seeking you first above all. Lord may your name be the first to remember and first to call out too, in good and in bad time.

Father God I pray and ask you for the strength to go through the trails and storm that I am facing and experiencing in my life. Lord I pray for the strength to rejoice in the trail I am facing. Father God I pray that the joy of the Lord will be my strength and my source of comfort.

Father God I faithfully ask for your help. Guide me through these storms of life, and help me to remember that you alone are the way, the truth and the light. Lord Jesus stay with me in times when I feel there is no end to the pain I feel.

Lord Jesus help me to remember, you too carried a heavy cross and yet you persevered. You knew our God had a plan, and that is what he intended for each and every one of us, even though we may not understand that by looking to you, we obtain the wisdom and love that will complete us. This I pray receive and declare in the mighty name of our Lord Jesus Christ, Amen. All the glory, honor and praise is your now and forever. Thank you Lord Jesus.

We have authority and dominion on the earth

Genesis 1:26 (KJV) And God said, Let us make man in our image, after our likeness; and let them have dominion over the fish of the sea, and over the fowl of the air, and over the cattle, and over all the earth, and over every creeping thing that creepeth upon the earth.

God give you and me something special; he gave us the authority over everything on the earth. He never gave it the angels or Lucifer, but he gave it to you and me. God is the author and finisher of the whole universe.

In the beginning when God created man, he gave man everything, the power, dominion and the authority to rule over everything on the earth; however, man had been deceive and by this deception man had given away the authority that God have given him.

There is still hope and faith in the God of our Lord Jesus Christ for those who believe in him; you want to know why because God send Jesus into the world as a human being. Therefore, Jesus could restore the given power and authority that God have given to man from the beginning of time.

We are born leaders, we are sons and daughters of the king of kings and the Lord of Lords. We are created in the image and likeness of

God; when God said let make man like him. He is saying you and me are special to him and he love us that much to create you and me in him image and likeness.

There is power in the name of Jesus, use that name, believe in his name, do not let anyone stop you from believing in the name of Jesus.

Jesus said the ones who believe in him name shall not perish but have eternal life. In addition, those who believe in him they may have to go through many trials but take to heart. Jesus said that it is finish he already overcome the world.

There is nothing to fear. Only have faith and believe in the one who send Jesus and believe in Jesus; there is no other way, Jesus is the only way to our heavenly father.

Therefore, no one can show you any other way to our Lord Jesus. Many will come in the name of Jesus, and many will use the name of Jesus, saying that they are massagers from God.

Jesus said test every spirit that claims that they come from God. There is a god of this world and there is our God from our Lord Jesus Christ; do not get mix up with the two. When many will say that they believe in God, ask them this question which god do you believe in, depend on their answer? Then you will know the tree by its fruit.

Likewise, not everyone who says that they believe in God is from God. The devil is a god for those who do not believe in the name of Jesus Christ.

Moreover, not everyone who says Lord, Lord will enter in to the kingdom of God; it will be the ones who believe, receive and do the will of God.

The devil can disguise himself in an angel of light, so be aware of that, because he is roaming the earth to see whom he can devour.

The light of our Lord Jesus Christ will continue to shine for all to see, all you have to do is call out to him and believe, he will help you. Jesus is our provider, our strength, our rock, our light, our savior and our deliver.

The light of the Lord is on the mountaintop where we can see him. It is not under a rock; his light is in all of us. If you have not repent and believe in the name of our Lord Jesus Christ today is the time to do it.

There is a saying it is better to be safe than sorry. No one is here to save you or me; no one can save you or me. The only one that can save us is our Lord Jesus Christ. That is why he came into this world. He came to redeem us by setting the captives free.

Jesus is here as a light for us to see our way through this dark world. Jesus is the light of the world and those who have that light is the light and salt of the world.

If you do not know Jesus, the Holy Bible is where you will get to know him, by reading and in prayer. The words of God are a light for those who read it and they will get know more of him.

The wages of sin is death and the gift of life from God is free and it is eternal; the gift of life was given to everyone through God son Jesus Christ. It is your choice to believe it and receive it.

I will not fear what they will try to do to you and me. Jesus said they cannot touch the soul. They may hurt the body that is all they can do, remember Jesus said it is finish.

Moreover, our help and strength comes from the Lord. I know we are not fighting against flesh and blood but against spirit, this is a spiritual battle.

However, the enemy will always try to tell you and me something different from what God of our Lord Jesus has said. Our Lord Jesus Christ will always come through to help us when we call out to him.

In this life, many of us will fail before we can even try. The words of God are sharper than any two-edge sword. It can cut through anything. That is how powerful our Lord is.

That is why we need to use the word of God, and his given power to do his will by (preaching and spreading the true gospel throughout the world and with love for each other. The true gospel of the kingdom of God.

You and I eternity depends on our willingness to understand and believe the true gospel! The apostle Paul warned the Christians of this day, for if he who preaches another Jesus whom we have not preached, or if you receive a different spirit which you have not received, or a different gospel which you have not accepted- you may well put up with it.

2 Corinthians 11: 13-15 (NIV) These people are false apostles. They are deceitful workers who disguise themselves as apostles of Christ. But I am not surprised! Even Satan disguises himself as servants of righteousness. In the end, they will get the punishment their wicked deeds deserve.

Frankly speaking, millions of sincere men and women have put up with a false gospel. They have been deceived all right- far too easily deceived.

1 Thessalonians 5:21 (NIV) But test everything that is said. Hold on to what is good.

Why, because too many have failed to obey God's command to prove all things.

Mark 1:15 (KJV) And saying, the time is fulfilled, and the kingdom of God is at hand; repent ye, and believe in the gospel.

Have you believe the same gospel, which Jesus preached? you need to be sure! there are many, many gospels being preached in the world today! Have you ever heard something like this?

Ephesians 6:12 (NIV) For we are not fighting struggle against flesh and blood enemies, but against the evil rulers and authorities of the unseen world, against mighty powers in this dark world, and against evil spirit in the heavenly places.

James 4:7 (KJV) Submit yourselves therefore to God. Resist the devil, and he will flee from you.

John 16; 33 (NIV) I have told you all this so that you may have peace in me. Here on earth you will have many trials and sorrows. But take heart, because I have overcome the world.

1 John 5: 4 (KJV) For whatsoever is born of God overcometh the world; and this is the victory that overcometh the world, even our faith.

Jesus gave you and me the authority over the enemy; Luke 10: 19 (NIV) Look, I have given you authority over all the power of the enemy, and you can walk among snakes and scorpions and crush them. Nothing will injure you.

Do not give the devil an opportunity; Ephesians 6:10-11 (NIV) A final word: Be strong in the Lord and in his mighty power. Put on all of God's armor so that you will be able to stand firm against all strategies of the devil.

God given wisdom is the only true wisdom.

Thank You

I would like to thank the God of our Lord Jesus Christ for his wisdom, understanding, peace, strength, knowledge, faith, hope, life, discernment and the gift of love to share with you. I Hope this message has giving everyone who read this some knowledge and awareness on your journey.

Whatever you are going through in life always, remember that where there is a will there is a way. Jesus is the way the truth and the life.

Seek him first in all that you do. He will never leave you or forsake you. You are not alone and you will never be alone. When there seems to be no way, you can call upon the name of Jesus Christ and he will make a way for you.

Moreover, always remember that you and I are made in the image and likeness of God. God so loved the world that he gave his only son Jesus Christ as a ransom.

They say failure is not an option; failure should be an option, because when you fail you can get right back up and try again.

This life is a test and a trial. We have to try and fail before we fail to try.

We are no longer living in a time of promise, but in the days of fulfillment. The word of God works, but we need to work God words.

We are not just here. We are not the skin. We are the breath that lives within.

We are all created equal; it is the choices that we make and the choices we let others influence us into making.

It is good to be thought of as a person and not a thing. Do not let your heart be trouble but let your heart be at peace. Jesus Christ said that he is the door. Do not worry about what anyone may think about you and the way they see you. We are living in a world where we as human being, are being process as things, instead of a people.

Jesus loves you just as you are; do not look at the negative in the world look at the promises of God and who he say you are.

There is a saying slavery is a sin when you know what to do when it is right and do not do it. God way missing the mark.

The whole concept of the western mind is to fight to survive. They say survival of the fittest.

They say life is a struggle; it is a struggle because death is taken as the opposite of life. When death should be a part of life.

Once you understand that death is not the opposite of life but part of it; which can never be separated from each other.

John 12:24 (KJV) Verily, verily, I say unto you, except a corn of wheat fall into the ground and die, it abides alone: but if it due, it bringeth forth much fruit.

Not Religious

They say whatever you believe is alright; however everybody has their own beliefs. Just so, they can believe something.

These are saying which you will hear from many people today; that their church and religion is the best way of teaching the truth. They sound nice, and help to make people feel good, since their own beliefs are said to be as valid as those of anyone else.

After all, some say, can you really know anything for sure? People who claim to have the truth are looked down upon as being arrogant and intolerant. For some reason, people can accept the idea that any religion is valid as long as it doesn't claim to be the only true religion! One of the greatest lies that Satan has foisted on human race is that religion can save you.

Do you know why that is? It's Satan's way of getting people to believe anything but the one thing that will remove his grip on the soul.

It is not true that all religious beliefs are of equal value. It is not true that whatever you believe is alright. The very fact that everybody has his or her own beliefs is what God says is man's biggest problem. We have exchanged his truth for our beliefs.

All of us are like sheep gone astray; we have turned everyone to his own way. Man has confused religions and stand in opposition to God's simple way to life. Man ways are the wide, tolerant, sin ignoring way that ends in destruction. Broad is the way that leadeth to destruction, narrow is the way that leadeth unto life and few there will find it.

There is one sense in which it is true that what you believe doesn't matter. What you believe, or what religious men have taught, does not change the truth of God's words! Just believing something doesn't make it so. Jumping off the top of a skyscraper onto the street below will kill you, no matter how strongly you believe otherwise.

Entering into eternity with the firm belief that there is no God, or that your beliefs or words are good enough to merit his approval will not change the outcome.

Whosoever, was not found written in the book of life was cast into the lake of fire.

Truth is not a matter of opinion. Either something is true or false. Jesus Christ claims to be the truth. He did not say I am a way, but rather, I am the way, the truth, and the life: no man cometh unto the father, but by me.

When it comes to faith, it is not, just so you believe Christ. Faith in Jesus Christ, who laid down his life on the cross of Calvary and rose victoriously from the dead, is the only way to everlasting life and forgiveness of sins.

Jesus as everyone has turned to his own way, each of us must individually turn from our rebellion. No one can save himself, since salvation is not of works. Because God is the one who saves, salvation is as certain as his promise:

He that heareth my word, and believe on him that sent me, hath everlasting life and shall not come into condemnation, but passed from death unto life.

Religion cannot save you because to enter God's eternal kingdom you need the new birth by the Holy Spirit.

Jesus Christ is the only way. Won't you stop rejecting him, and by faith receive him as your savior today. Neither is there salvation in any other. For there is none other name under heaven given among men, whereby we must be saved.

Hebrews 13:8 (NIV) Jesus Christ is the same yesterday, today, and forever.

Gift From God

In this day and time, it's not often that someone offers an absolutely free gift. Yet here is the most wonderful and precious gift especially for you!

It has already been paid for by someone else. This gift is eternal life in a glorious Heaven. It is difficult for men to accept the thought of this being a free gift. Man wants to earn everlasting life.

The Holy Bible says: for by grace are ye saved through faith; and that not of yourselves: it is the gift of God: not of works, lest any man should boast. The Bible says: the gift of God is eternal life through Jesus Christ our Lord.

A gift is not something we earn or work for. We receive gifts out of love. In fact, Grace means unmerited, or unearned favor. If we work for something, it is not a gift, but a wage.

There is only one spiritual wage a person can obtain. The wage of sin is death.

Romans 6:23 (NIV) For the wages of sin is death, but the free gift of God is eternal life through Jesus Christ our Lord.

The Lord Jesus Christ paid for this gift with his own dear shed blood on the cross, without shedding of blood is no remission. The blood of Jesus Christ, God son cleanse us from all sin.

God commend his love towards us, in that, whole we were yet sinners, Christ died for us.

Receive this absolutely free gift today! Come to God in humble prayer, admit your guilt as a sinner before a Holy God, and turn to God from your sin by faith (repent), asking God to save you through the Lord Jesus Christ.

As many as received him, to them gave the power to become the sons of God, even to them that believe on his name; testifying both to the Jew, and to the Greeks, repentance toward God, and faith toward our Lord Jesus Christ.

Romans 10:13 (NIV) For everyone who calls on the name of the Lord will be saved. Remember faith comes by hearing, and hearing by the word of God.

Our Life Is The Purpose

Ecclesiastes 12:13 (KJV) Let us hear the conclusion of the whole matter. Fear God, and keep his commandments. For this is the whole duty of man.

We are living in a world where we as people are looking for a purpose and a meaning to be someone and to do something. In order to be accepted by others.

Is there a purpose in life for us as human being, or our life is the purpose. We are living in a time where the western new age lifestyle system wants us as people to adopt too.

They want us to become something or someone other than who God have created us to be. God created you and me to be in his image and his likeness. Many of us have change our identity by doing the opposite from what God has said to do.

The world teaches many of us who listen to the world that we need to find a purpose in life. They don't teach us that our life is the purpose.

The devil's purpose in the past was to keep Christ away from the world; having failed that goal the only option left to him is to keep the world away from Christ.

Satan has sprinkle lies with half-truths to create doubt in our minds and about the faithfulness and glory of God.

Satan has blinded people minds. Lest the light of the gospel of the glory of Christ who is the image of God, should shine on them.

God did not give Satan the world to rule; Satan wrested it from the hands of Adam and Eve.

Paul says in 2 Corinthians 11:14 (NIV) But I am not surprised! Even Satan disguises himself as an angel of light.

Satan have deceives many by hiding the hideous nature of sin under a facade of attractiveness; Satan original name, Lucifer, mean star of the morning. Who is Satan; he is the evil one the scripture speak about; the accuser, the father of all lies who is trying to keep us from being who God had created you and me to be.

Satan tempts us to sin and tries to keep us from believing in God. He is our opponent. We don't see him, but he is there.

Jesus himself prayed for us that the father would keep us from the evil one.

We should not be afraid of him, but he does exist stay focus on who you are in Christ. Greater is he who is in you is greater than he who is in the world.

Moreover, put on the whole Amor of protection from God and use the sword of the spirit against the lies that Satan is using.

In the beginning when Satan deceive Adam and Eve his business was to employ Adam and Eve to do his purpose and not be the purpose of life that God had created them to be.

He wanted them to find a purpose in life, when there life was already the purpose.

We are not of this world, so we should not do and be what the world is doing.

John 17:16 (KJV) They are not of the world, even as I am not of the world.

John 15:19 (KJV) If ye were of the world, the world would love his own; but because ye are not of the world, but I have chosen you out of the world, therefore the world hateth you.

Satan is and will try to make something look like the truth when it is a lie. He will tell you that God does not love you because of what you have done wrong. One of his lies, that God is so disappointed in you; that he will give up on you and he do not love you.

You may be thinking, God does not really love me, if God loves me, I would not be having all these problems. That may feel like the truth, but it is not. Jesus said, as the father has loved me, so have I loved you.

This is love, not that we loved God, but that he loved us. See how great a love the father has bestowed on us, that we would be called children of God, and such we are.

Do not fall for the lies from the devil anymore.

God loves you and me so much that he gave his life through Jesus Christ. We are asset not liability, we are God masterpiece. That is why God created you and me in his image and his likeness.

We often look to numbers and out word, achievements, but God sees things differently. Stay focused on obedience to what God has told you to do and don't compare yourself with others.

Measure success by obedience not out word success. God sees your worth and rejoice in it.

Success is feeling good about who I am and what I am to others, not what others think of me but what Jesus know about me.

I have fullness in Christ; Colossians 2:10 (NIV) So you also are complete through your union with Christ, who is the head over every ruler and authority.

Giving Thanks To The Lord

I pray in the name that God our heavenly father has given to you and me. The name that is above every other name Jesus Christ.

I prayer that every person hands that pick up this book, and every eyes that read this message and every ear that hear the words of God with be fill with His Holy Spirit; in Jesus name.

I pray that God with fill our mind with his wisdom, understanding and knowledge to know the truth and that the truth will set us free; In Jesus name.

I pray that every heart that read this message with repent, confess and believe in the God of our Lord Jesus Christ. I pray that you will receive Jesus Christ into your heart and make him your Lord and savior.

I pray that every life with be renew, body, mind, spirit and soul with be fill with the grace and glory form God.

I pray that you will find peace in your life and joy in every breath you take. I pray that God blessing with be with you everywhere you go; in your going out and in your coming in.

I pray that any weapon and tongue that rise and speak against us shall not prosper; in the name of Jesus Christ.

Father God in heaven, in the name of Jesus Christ, I believe that Jesus died on the cross for my sin and raised again form the dead.

I confess all my sins and repent. I forgive everyone who had hurt and done me wrong. Father God, please forgive me as I forgive myself.

Heavenly father, I ask of you, to breath your breathe in me; and fill me with your Holy Spirit, as I receive your son Jesus Christ into my life as my Lord and savior.

I renounce every deceptive spirit that came against my mom, my dad, my first family members and myself in the past life in the name of Jesus Christ.

I pray that we will have a sound mind, a faithful spirit and a loving heart.

I pray that the light of the Lord will always be with us and that his love will continue to shine through you and me forever.

I pray that God will make a way when there seems not to be a way. I pray that we will find the strength in every area of our lives; in the name of Jesus Christ.

I pray that we will always seek God first in everything that we do and say. I pray that God will answer our prayers. I pray that God will be our mouthpiece and our guide.

I pray that we will help those who are in the need of our help; I pray that our lives with be fruitful. I pray that all will be saved; in the name of Jesus Christ.

I pray that we will find comfort in those we comfort and those who will comfort us. I pray that we will be faithful in the storm.

I pray that we will always be grateful for everything that we have in our lives. I pray that we will never give up but stay faithful no matter what may happen. We are not alone and we will never be alone; God is always here with us, we may not see him or feel him, but he is there. Trust me.

I pray that we will always listen, obey God commandments, and do his will.

We are God temple that is why we should take care of his temple and live holy lives. Holiness is not only a possibility for the Christian; holiness is requirement. Without holiness, no one will see the Lord.

In the name of Jesus Christ and to God be the glory, May his peace and love be with us all. Thank you Lord all the glory, the honor, the praises and worship goes to you, in Jesus Christ I pray.

We Were Born To Be Worshipper And To Have A Relationship With Our Creator

In today's world, we see many people worshiping the things in the world; but not so much of the God that created the whole universe. There are true worshiper and false worshiper in this time and age that we are living in. Therefore, you should be aware of who is and who is not. Jesus said they worship me with their mouth but their heart is far from me.

God created the world for his own glory. Man and woman were created to have a relationship with their creator through prayers and worship.

In the beginning when our heavenly father created Adam and Eve and put them in the Garden of Eden; God would come and visit Adam and Eve every day and they would have fellowship with their creator.

1 John 3:1 (NIV) See how very much our father loves us, for he calls us his children, and that is what we are! But the people who belong to this world don't recognize that we are God's because they don't know him.

Adam and Eve got distracted and did something that God tell them not to do, but still did it. After realizing what they had done, they were hiding themselves; then the eyes of both of them were opened, and they *realized they were naked; so they sewed fig leaves together and made coverings for themselves.*

Then the man and his wife heard the sound of the Lord God as he was walking in the Garden in the cool of the day, and they hid from God among the trees of the garden. However, the Lord God called to the man, where are you.

He answered, I heard you in the garden, and I was afraid because I was naked; so I hid. The story continues in Genesis 3:11 (NIV)

After all had said by God to Adam and Eve, Adam and his wife Eve were put out of the Garden of Eden. They had lost that spiritual relationship, and bond that they had with their creator. The enemy of our creator distracted Adam and his wife Eve. However, God had a plan in the future for us, so that man can restore the relationship they once had with him through our Lord Jesus Christ.

However, many things have change from then to now with the same distraction but in a different form. The enemy is trying to keep us away from having a relationship with our heavenly father.

There is so much distraction in the world today; that man is being distracted from their walk with Jesus Christ.

One of the biggest distractions in the world today for human being is the media. The devil is using the things in the world; he is trying to keep us from having a relationship with our creator. It is so easy to get caught up in the media.

When I say media, I am referring to the internet, TV, movies, music, video game, newspapers and magazines.

As I said, the media is so dangerous because it is so easy to get consumed in the things that it portrays.

The media is trying to convince us that we are missing something, and they are the ones that can fill the need. Everywhere we turn, some sort of media is right in our face.

We are slowly being bombard by the media with how we should look, feel, live and act. Example with the movies, the music, the TV shows etc.

We should not let the things of the world defile who we are and who we should be. The things that they are portraying through these devices, they are filled with filth.

They are all horrible influences on us because they can subliminally tell us how to live, what is right and what is wrong.

I am not saying that you should or should not watch TV, movies and listen to music. It is what you are watching and listening to. We all have a choice in what we let in through our gateways. So stop feeding the flesh and start feeding the spirit.

There are many things in the world that many of us are being consumed by; many of us are not aware of the attachment and distraction that these things are causing in our lives.

Many of us are becoming so attach and dependent on the things in the world. I am not saying not to use the things in the world; all I am saying is to not get to attach and lose yourselves in it.

We are so caught up into the things of the world; that we don't even talk to people as we did before.

We become so lazy and comfortable. We need to build up each other iron sharpen iron.

Many us are worshiping and have relationships with the things of the world instead of your creator and others.

Likewise we do not talk to people vocally as we use too, we text. Being friend with the world is being an enemy to God.

1 John 2:15-17 (NIV)) Do not love this world nor the things it offers you, for when you love the world, you do not have the love of the father in you.

For the world offers only a craving for physical pleasure, a craving for everything we see, and pride in our achievements and possessions. These are not from the father, but are from this world.

And this world is fading away, along with everything that people crave. But anyone who does what pleases God will live forever.

We are by our nature, sinful, and if we live by our nature, we will not get close to God. That is why we need to die to ourselves, and live in Christ.

However, no matter what we do, there will be a constant battle within ourselves between spirit and flesh.

That is why we need to constantly allow God to search our hearts, and purify it. The first step to overcoming ourselves is being aware.

It is a constant struggle to keep our eyes fixed on Jesus, and to not become distracted by the passing concerns and things of this world.

Nevertheless, if we are aware of what can, and does, interfere with our walks with God, we can begin to take the necessary actions to prevent them.

Remember, Matthew 6:33 (KJV) Seek ye first the kingdom of God, and his righteousness; and all these things shall be added to unto you.

We need to start listening more of what our heavenly father is saying before we speak. Let us come together in prayers and worship our heavenly in spirit and in truth.

So you must remain faithful to what you have been taught from the beginning. If you do, you will remain in fellowship with the son and the father. And in this fellowship we enjoy the eternal life he promised us.

For the spirit teaches everything you need to know, and what he teaches is true- it is not a lie. So just as he has taught you, remain in fellowship with Christ. Be in the word of our heavenly father and let his words be in you.

May the Holy Spirit of our heavenly father be with us all now and forever. In the mighty and powerful name of our Lord Jesus Christ. The name that was given above all names, the only name that we can be saved by. God bless you. There is power in the name of Jesus Christ. Use it and receive it now. Remember everything begins in the spirit. Obey God's commandments to believe, have faith and to love each other. Thank you Lord.